Trash to TREASURE

You've been to the flea markets, visited garage sales, even cleaned out the attic — now it's time to bring new life to things old and forgotten! Let us show you how to transform set-aside, handed-down, "seen-better-days" items into exciting home décor, one-of-a-kind handmade gifts, and dazzling keepsakes. This volume of Trash to Treasure *is filled with furniture and fabric makeovers, unique room accessories, and delightful decorations transformed from discards and throwaways. From fun and simple to fancy and elegant, here are 90+ economical, easy-to-do projects …
an entirely new crafting adventure just for you!*

Anne Childs

LEISURE ARTS, INC.
Little Rock, Arkansas

EDITORIAL STAFF

Vice-President and Editor-at-Large: Anne Van Wagner Childs
Vice-President and Editor-in-Chief: Sandra Graham Case
Director of Designer Relations: Debra Nettles
Design Director: Cyndi Hansen
Editorial Director: Susan Frantz Wiles
Publications Director: Kristine Anderson Mertes
Creative Art Director: Gloria Bearden
Photography Director: Karen Hall
Art Operations Director: Jeff Curtis

DESIGN
Senior Designers: Polly Tullis Browning, Diana Sanders Cates, Cherece Athy Cooper, and Jennifer Todd
Designers: Sandra Spotts Ritchie, Billie Steward, Anne Pulliam Stocks, Linda Diehl Tiano, and Becky Werle
Executive Assistant: Debra Smith

TECHNICAL
Managing Editors: Theresa Hicks Young and Barbara Marguerite McClintock
Technical Writers: Sherry Solida Ford and Leslie Schick Gorrell
Copy Editors: Susan Frazier and Kimberly J. Smith
Production Assistant: Sharon Gillam

EDITORIAL
Managing Editor: Suzie Puckett
Associate Editors: Ashley Michael, Jennifer L. Riley, and Taryn L. Stewart

ART
Art Director: Mark Hawkins
Graphic Artists: Elaine Barry and Mark Potter
Photography Stylists: Tiffany Huffman and Janna Laughlin
Staff Photographer: Russell Ganser
Publishing Systems Administrator: Becky Riddle
Publishing Systems Assistants: Myra Means and Chris Wertenberger

PROMOTIONS
Managing Editor: Alan Caudle
Associate Editor: Steven M. Cooper
Designer: Dale Rowett
Graphic Artist: Deborah Kelly

BUSINESS STAFF

Publisher: Rick Barton
Vice President, Finance: Tom Siebenmorgen
Director of Corporate Planning and Development: Laticia Mull Cornett
Vice President, Retail Marketing: Bob Humphrey
Retail Marketing Director: Margaret Sweetin

Vice President, Sales: Ray Shelgosh
Vice President, National Accounts: Pam Stebbins
Vice President, Operations: Jim Dittrich
Comptroller, Operations: Rob Thieme
Retail Customer Service Manager: Wanda Price
Print Production Manager: Fred F. Pruss

Copyright© 2001 by Leisure Arts, Inc., 5701 Ranch Drive, Little Rock, Arkansas 72223-9633. All rights reserved. No part of this book may be reproduced in any form or by any means without the prior written permission of the publisher, except for brief quotations in reviews appearing in magazines or newspapers. We have made every effort to ensure that these instructions are accurate and complete. We cannot, however, be responsible for human error, typographical mistakes, or variations in individual work. Made in the United States of America.

Library of Congress Catalog Number 98-65089
Hardcover International Standard Book Number 1-57486-215-4

10 9 8 7 6 5 4 3 2 1

TABLE OF CONTENTS

second chances 6

KITCHEN CADDY 8
  Chest Kitchen Cart
CHILD'S "BUSY-CENTER" 10
  Child's Desk and Chair
COFFEE-TIME BENCH 12
  Coffee Table Bench
RUSTIC PAPER PARTITION 13
  Folding Screen Room Divider
FENCE-PICKET COAT RACK 14
  Fence-Picket Coat Rack
EYE-CATCHING END TABLE 16
  Piano Bench End Table
CHILD'S ART CENTER 18
  Chalkboard Table and Chair
BENCH SEATING 19
  Chair Bench
WINDOWPANE COFFEE TABLE 20
  Window Coffee Table
COTTAGE SHUTTER TABLE 22
  Shutter Table
SHADOW BOX TABLE 23
  Shadow Box Table
OLD-STYLE SETTEE 24
  Headboard Settee
A REFRESHING CHANGE 26
  Bathroom Organizer

creative touches 28

CREATIVE CLOTHESPIN FRAME 30
  Clothespin Frame
APPEALING PLATE RACK 32
  Plate Rack
"SEW" FUN NOTES 33
  Stationery Drawer Tote
CORRUGATED FLOOR LAMP 34
  Coffee Can Floor Lamp
CORK-POPPER'S MESSAGE BOARD 36
  Cork Bulletin Board
MAILBOX WASTEBASKET 37
  Mailbox Trash Can
PERKY LAMP 38
  Percolator Lamp
BELTED FOOTSTOOL 40
  Belted Footstool
"KEY TO MY HEART" FRAME 41
  Key To My Heart Frame
PICTURE-PERFECT SOFTWARE 42
  Computer Monitor Cover
NOTABLE CD HOLDER 44
  Shoebox CD Holder
TIME IN THE BALANCE 45
  Scale Clock
DAPPER DRAWER OTTOMAN 46
  Drawer Ottoman
OLD-FASHIONED FLAIR 48
  Doorknob Hanging Rack
GRAPEVINE NOTEBOX 49
  Designer Mailbox
GAS CAN LAMP 50
  Gas Can Lamp
SENSATIONAL SERVING TRAY 52
  Three-Tier Server
BATHING BEAUTIES 53
  Bath Oil Bottles
MOSAIC MASTERPIECE 54
  Eggshell Mosaic
FLASHY PHOTO TREE 56
  Camera Photo Tree
BEADED BEDAZZLERS 57
  Beaded Jars
COOKBOOK STAND 58
  Book Stand
DECOUPAGED BIRD PLAQUES 60
  Bird Plaques
"FAN" CLUB PHOTO SCREEN 61
  Fan Blade Photo Display

TABLE OF CONTENTS

creative touches (Continued) 28

CHEF'S GADGET LAMP 62
Kitchen Lamp
DISTINCTIVE MESSAGES 64
Framed Corkboard
GLOBAL LAMP 65
Globe Lampshade
POSTAL POCKETS 66
Mail Holder
HOT NEWS BOARD 68
Cookie Sheet Memo Holder
LADYBUG TRICYCLE 69
Painted Tricycle
COZY CABIN 70
Lighted Cabin
CORRUGATED FRAMES 72
Corrugated Cardboard Frames
PRETTY CANDLE PLATTER 73
Dried Flower Candle Dish
PILLOWCASE HANG-UP 74
Closet Organizer
BREAD BOX ORGANIZER 76
Bread Box Organizer

SEASIDE TREASURE BOX 77
Shadow Box Frame
THE LATEST BUZZ 78
Cabinet Door Message Center
TIMEWORN FRUIT TRAY 80
Weathered Fruit
STACKED-UP CAKE STAND 81
Cake Stand
STRAW MAT MAKEOVERS 82
Straw Ensemble
NOSTALGIC MAGAZINE RACK 84
Magazine Rack
SPICY JEWELRY RACK 85
Spice Rack Jewelry Organizer
"TEA-LIGHTFUL" LAMP 86
Teapot Lamp
PAGE-TURNING PRINTS 88
Children's Book Framed Print
"CAN-DID" FRAME 89
Beverage Can Frame

soft and simple 90

SHIRT-PATCH WRAP 92
Shirt Patchwork Quilt
SIMPLE SACHETS 94
Sachets
GOOD-NIGHT SACHETS 96
Nightie Sachet Bags
"WELL-SUITED" FRAME 97
Men's Suit Collage
GRACEFUL CHAIR COVERS 98
Chair Covers
PROM-DRESS PILLOWS 100
Prom-Dress Pillows
HANKIE TABLE TOPPER 102
Hankie Table Topper
PLACE MATS UNDERFOOT! 103
Place Mat Throw Rug

COUNTRY GARDEN CUSHION 104
Sock Appliqué Pillow
BABY'S KEEPSAKE QUILT 106
Baby's Wall Quilt
COMFY CHENILLE CUSHION 108
Chenille Pillow
SCALLOPED SHELF EDGING 109
Shelf Edging
PATCHWORK PILLOWS 110
Canvas Bag Pillows
VINTAGE DOILY PILLOW 112
Vintage Doily Pillow
DRAPERY TABLE MATS 114
Drapery Place Mats
SHIRT-POCKET ORGANIZER 115
Shirt-Pocket Wall Hanging

TABLE OF CONTENTS

a fresh approach 116

ROCK-A-BYE FLOWER BED 118
  Doll Cradle Planter
BUTTERFLY "DE-LIGHTS" 120
  Butterfly Patio Lights
PERKY PLANT HANG-UPS 121
  Coffee Can Plant Holders
CHILL OUT 122
  Patio Ice Bucket
LOVELY ILLUMINATION 123
  Brick Votive Holder
CANDLELIGHT DINING 124
  Chicken Feeder Candleholder
SPORTY GARDEN SCULPTURES 125
  Concrete Garden Ornaments
DANCING DRAGONFLY 126
  Copper Dragonfly
GAZING GLOBE 127
  Gazing Globe
TIERED TERRA-COTTA 128
  Tiered Planter
FLUTTERING FANCIES 129
  Flowerpot Windsocks
TERRA-COTTA CANDLEHOLDER 130
  Terra-cotta Candleholder
STENCILED SETTINGS 131
  Stenciled Table Topper
FLOATING CANDLELIGHT 132
  Floating Candleholder

CANDLELIGHT TOWERS 133
  Drinking-Glass Candleholders
GARDEN ELEGANCE 134
  Plant Pedestal
"INVISIBLE" PLANTER 135
  Tomato Cage Planter
FENCE-RAIL FLAG 136
  Fence Post Flag
GARDEN CANDLE SHIELD 137
  Shielded Candleholder
CHAIRBACK PLANTER 138
  Ladder-Back Chair Planter
GREAT SERVING CRATE 139
  Soda Crate Serving Tray
CANISTER TOPIARY 140
  Coffee Can Topiary
DRESSER-DRAWER PLANTER 141
  Drawer Planter
PERCOLATED POSY 142
  Percolated Posy
GARDEN BEAUTIES 144
  Garden Gate and Bench

PATTERNS 146
GENERAL INSTRUCTIONS 156
CREDITS 160

give new life to that long-forgotten piece of furniture with the touch of a paintbrush and the magic of your own imagination. Or bring the breath of creativity into your home with "new" room accessories crafted from timeworn discards. Amazing transformations from old headboards, hand-me-down chests, and set-aside chairs and tables are really quite simple with these innovative ideas for fun-to-do furniture makeovers.

KITCHEN CADDY

Transform an old chest of drawers into this handy kitchen caddy with a few simple painting techniques. The versatility and liveliness of this cute rolling chest make it a chef's delight in any kitchen.

CHEST KITCHEN CART

Recycled item: chest of drawers

You will also need ¼" plywood; saw; wood glue; hammer; ¾" long nails; ½"w wooden trim; sandpaper; miter box; four ⅜" x 2" long wood screws; two wooden decorative corner brackets; drill and bits; four wheel casters (optional); spray primer; white spray paint; white, yellow, red, light green, green, and dark green acrylic paint; paintbrushes; two 2" dia. ceramic knob facings; two 1¼" dia. round ceramic ball drawer pulls; wrought iron towel bar to fit end of chest; stencil plastic; craft knife; cutting mat; natural sponge; and clear acrylic spray sealer.

Allow wood glue, primer, paint, and sealer to dry after each application.

1. For shelves, remove desired number of drawers from chest.
2. For each shelf, cut a piece of plywood to fit inside chest. Glue shelves in chest along drawer supports; nail in place.
3. Cut a length of trim to fit along front edge of each shelf; sand ends smooth and nail in place.
4. Mitering corners, cut trim pieces to fit edges of drawer front. Glue and nail trims in place.
5. Use wood screws to attach decorative brackets to bottom front of chest.
6. If desired, follow manufacturer's instructions to attach casters to legs.
7. Apply primer to chest and drawers. Spray paint inside of chest, drawer, and shelves white. Paint outside of chest and corner brackets green.
8. Attach knob facings and knobs to drawer. Follow manufacturer's instructions to attach towel bar to one end of cart.
9. Trace radish and leaf patterns, page 147, onto stencil plastic; cut out.
10. Referring to *Stenciling*, page 157, paint radishes white. Allowing red paint to fade about half way down radish, paint radish tops red. Paint leaves green. Freehand dark green stems.
11. Apply two to three coats of sealer to cart.

CHILD'S "BUSY-CENTER"

Crafted from a table and wooden shelf, this attractive desk keeps art supplies and toys at arm's reach. Paint a chair in coordinating primary colors, and your busy bee will be all set for action!

CHILD'S DESK AND CHAIR

Recycled items: a child-size wooden table and chair and a wooden bookshelf to fit on table

You will also need a saw, sandpaper, tack cloth, primer, desired colors of acrylic paint, paintbrushes, four 1" "L" brackets, and clear acrylic sealer.

Refer to Painting Techniques, page 157, before beginning project. Allow primer, paint, and sealer to dry after each application.

1. Cut bottom from shelf leaving desired height for hutch.
2. Sand hutch, table, and chair; wipe with tack cloth.
3. Use brackets to attach hutch to table (Fig. 1).

Fig. 1

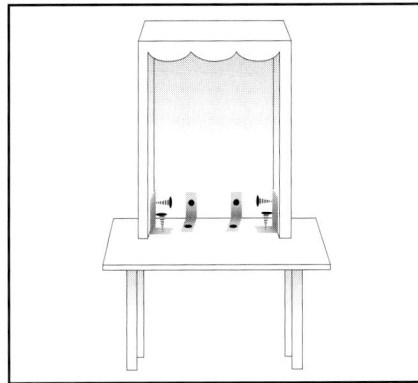

4. Apply primer to desk and chair.
5. Paint desk and chair basecoat colors; paint dots and checkerboards as desired.
6. Apply two to three coats of sealer to desk and chair.

Coffee-Time Bench

This attractive padded bench, crafted out of a wooden coffee table, provides a comfortable place to prop your feet up while sipping your morning java. It can also be used as extra seating for drop-by guests.

Coffee Table Bench

Recycled item: wooden coffee table frame with glass removed

You will also need desired basecoat and brown acrylic paint, paintbrushes, paste floor wax, sandpaper, ³⁄₄" plywood, 4"-thick foam, batting, fabric to cover foam, and a staple gun.

1. Paint frame desired color; allow to dry. Apply wax to edges of frame, then wipe with a soft cloth. Working in small sections, paint frame brown; wipe immediately with a soft cloth. Lightly sand frame.
2. For cushion, cut pieces from plywood and foam to fit frame.
3. Cut pieces from batting and fabric 15" larger than foam piece. Place fabric wrong side up on a flat surface. Place batting on fabric. Center foam, then plywood on batting. Wrap short edges of fabric to back of plywood; staple in place. Squaring corners, repeat to secure long fabric edges to plywood.
4. Place cushion on bench.

RUSTIC PAPER PARTITION

Whether used to divide a room or shield unsightly clutter, this convenient folding screen is a natural! You'll find it effortless to craft this attractive partition by "sewing" handmade paper panels to a room divider and gluing on preserved fern fronds.

FOLDING SCREEN ROOM DIVIDER

Recycled item: folding screen with dowels to hold fabric inserts

You will also need wood-tone spray, handmade paper (we used six 24½" x 36½" pieces of paper), ⅛" dia. hole punch, liquid fray preventive, raffia, spray adhesive, and preserved fern fronds.

Allow wood-tone spray, fray preventive, and spray adhesive to dry after each application.

1. Remove fabric from dowels and discard.
2. Apply wood-tone spray to frame.
3. Measure inside width and length of each section between top and bottom dowels. Piecing as necessary, cut pieces from paper the determined measurements.
4. Punch holes 1" apart and 1" from top and bottom of each paper piece. Apply fray preventive to each hole. Overlapping edges and knotting raffia at ends to secure, use one strand of raffia to lace paper pieces together.
5. Applying spray adhesive to one side of each fern frond, arrange on paper pieces and smooth in place.
6. Position each laced paper piece in frame. Use raffia to sew each end of paper pieces to dowel through holes.

FENCE-PICKET COAT RACK

Rather than building a fence to keep the neighbors out, welcome them into your home with this interesting coat rack. Simply assemble four fence pickets for the 6-foot post, and you'll create a coat rack that will certainly entice visitors to take off their coats and stay awhile.

FENCE-PICKET COAT RACK

Recycled items: four 1" x 4" x 12" boards and four 1" x 4" x 6' fence pickets

You will also need a dinner plate, coping or jig saw, drill with $1/4$" drill bit, wood glue, eight 6" long "C" clamps, $1\,1/4$" long wood screws, white and green acrylic paint, paintbrushes, paste floor wax, sandpaper, tack cloth, clear acrylic spray sealer, and brass coat hooks.

Allow wood glue, paint, wax, and sealer to dry after each application. Drill a pilot hole before applying screws.

1. For each foot, refer to Fig. 1 and use plate to draw a curve at one end of each 12" board. Use saw to cut each board along drawn line. Mark and drill holes in board.

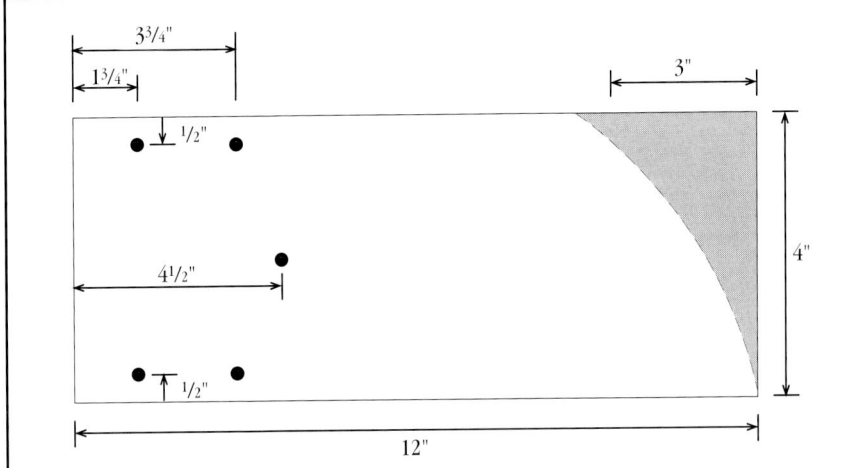

Fig. 1

2. Referring to Fig. 2, glue pickets together to form a post, using clamps to hold in place. Spacing 12" apart, drive screws along overlapped edges of boards to secure.

Fig. 2

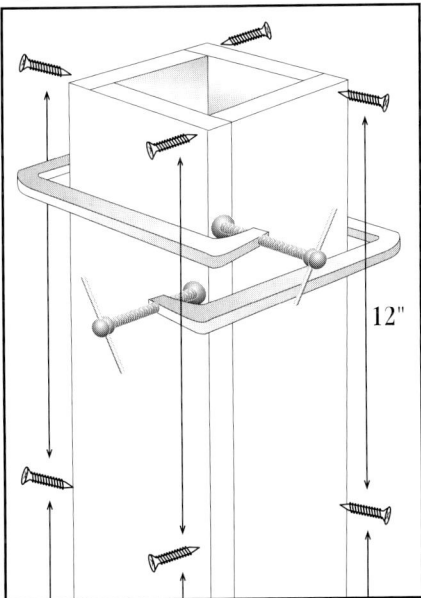

3. Aligning edges of feet with edges of post, use screws to attach feet to post.

4. Paint coat rack green. Lightly apply wax along edges of rack, then paint white. Sand waxed areas and wipe with tack cloth. Apply two to three coats of sealer to rack.

5. Follow manufacturer's instructions to attach hooks to rack.

Eye-Catching End Table

Transform that neglected piano bench into a handy end table and use it to stash away your television remote and program guide. We decorated ours with eye-catching geometric diamonds, but you can paint yours to match any décor!

PIANO BENCH END TABLE

Recycled item: piano bench with hinged top

You will also need a saw, four 2" long hinges, sandpaper, tack cloth, ecru and green acrylic paint, paintbrushes, clear contact paper, gold medium-point paint pen, and clear acrylic spray sealer.

Allow paint, paint pen, and sealer to dry after each application.

1. Remove top from bench; remove and discard hardware. Draw a parallel line 7" from one short edge on bench top. Cut top apart along drawn line. Use two hinges to reattach large top piece to bench. Placing remaining hinges along outside short edge of bench, hinge small top piece to bench.
2. Sand bench top and wipe with tack cloth; paint ecru.
3. Referring to Fig. 1, draw a light line down center of bench lengthwise and widthwise.
4. Trace diamond pattern, page 151, onto contact paper twelve times (number may vary depending on bench size); cut out diamonds.
5. Beginning at center and working outward and trimming diamonds as necessary, refer to Fig. 1 to place and smooth diamonds on bench top.

Fig. 1

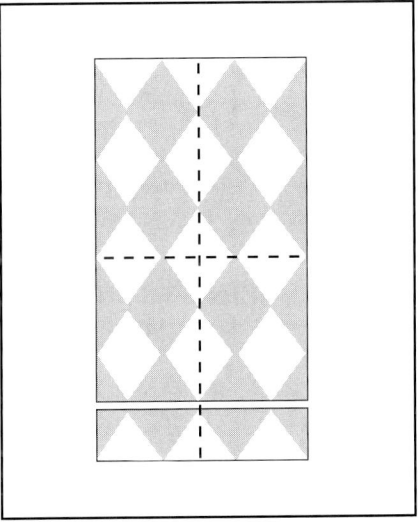

6. Paint areas between diamonds green. Remove contact paper and erase lines on top. Lightly sand top and wipe with tack cloth. Use paint pen to draw a swirl at center of ecru diamonds.
7. Apply two to three coats of sealer to top.

CHILD'S ART CENTER

Encourage your little artist to "color outside the lines" with a child-size activity center. A spacious, spray-on chalkboard tabletop will foster experimentation without sacrificing the finish on your home's furniture and walls!

CHALKBOARD TABLE AND CHAIR

Recycled items: a child-size wooden table and chair

You will also need sandpaper, tack cloth, spray primer, black chalkboard spray paint, desired colors of acrylic paint, paintbrushes, and clear acrylic spray sealer.

Refer to Painting Techniques, page 157, before beginning project. Allow primer, paint, and sealer to dry after each application.

1. If necessary, sand table and chair; wipe with tack cloth.
2. Apply primer to table and chair.
3. Spray top of table with black paint (more than one coat may be necessary for desired coverage).
4. Paint remainder of table and chair as desired.
5. Cover chalkboard top of table; apply two to three coats of sealer to remainder of table and to chair.

BENCH SEATING

Have you been playing musical chairs while attempting to seat guests for your garden parties? The solution to your "growing" problem is this cleverly crafted bench! A fabric tablecloth and a foam rubber pad transform a pair of ladder-back chairs into comfortable seating.

CHAIR BENCH

Recycled items: two wooden ladder-back chairs with slat seats and a fabric tablecloth

You will also need a saw; one 1" x 4", one 1" x 8", and two 1" x 6" boards; drill with $1/16$" dia. bit; wood glue; #6 x $1 1/4$" long coarse-thread drywall screws; wood filler; sandpaper; spray primer; white spray paint; clear acrylic spray sealer; 2" thick foam rubber piece, and fabric to coordinate with tablecloth.

Use a $1/16$" dia. bit and drill to make a pilot hole for each screw. Fill each hole with glue before applying screw.

1. Remove slats from seats of chairs and set aside; place chairs facing each other.
2. For seat, cut two 48" long pieces from 1" x 6" boards. If necessary, put wooden spacers between back seat rungs and seat boards to level; use screws to attach seat boards to chair rungs.
3. For backrest, cut pieces from 1" x 6" and 1" x 4" boards to fit across back of bench. If desired, slightly angle-cut ends of boards to accommodate slant of chairback. Use screws to secure backboards to bench.
4. For shelf, cut a piece from 1" x 8" board to fit bottom of bench. Use screws to attach shelf to bottom chair rungs.
5. Use screws to attach slats to front of bench.
6. Use wood filler to cover screw heads; when dry, sand. Allowing to dry after each application, apply primer, two to three coats of spray paint, then sealer to entire bench.
7. For seat cushion, cut a piece from foam rubber to fit seat.
8. For seat cover, measure width and length of seat cushion; add 4" to each measurement. Cut one piece each from tablecloth and fabric the determined measurements. Matching right sides and short edges and using a $1/2$" seam allowance, sew long edges and one short edge together. Press remaining raw edges $1/2$" to wrong side twice; topstitch in place.
8. Turn seat cover right side out; place seat cushion in cover, then place on bench.

WINDOWPANE COFFEE TABLE

Gain a new view with a clever, window-frame coffee table. A colorful quilt top adds a quaint touch to this eye-catching conversation piece.

WINDOW COFFEE TABLE

Recycled items: window with wooden frame (our window has diagonal decorative panes) and a piece of quilt top to fit window

You will also need a saw, ¼" plywood, staple gun, small brads, 1" x 4" lumber, small finishing nails, wood glue, 1¾" long flat-head wood screws, four 14" long table legs, sandpaper, tack cloth, masking tape, primer, acrylic paint, paintbrushes, and clear acrylic spray sealer.

Allow wood glue, primer, paint, and sealer to dry after each application.

1. Measure length and width of window; cut one piece of quilt and plywood the determined measurements.
2. Place quilt on plywood; staple ¼" from edges to secure. Place plywood quilt side down on window. Using small brads, nail plywood to window frame.
3. Cut pieces of 1" x 4" lumber to fit ends of window; glue, then nail in place. Cut pieces of lumber to fit sides of window; glue, then nail in place.
4. Use screws to attach one table leg to each corner of table.
5. Sand table; wipe with tack cloth. Mask off glass, then apply primer and two coats of paint to table. Apply two to three coats of sealer to table.

Cottage Shutter Table

This charming table is ideal for a cozy reading corner. Simply use hinges to connect two sets of old shutters and top with a square piece of wood. A crackled paint finish adds to the quaint cottage look.

Shutter Table

Recycled items: two sets of wooden shutters (each of our shutter sections measure 9"w x 27"h)

You will also need a drill and bits; 1" long "L" brackets; wood glue; 18" square piece of wood for tabletop; ecru spray paint; crackle medium; ecru and brown acrylic paint; paintbrushes; and clear acrylic spray sealer.

Allow glue, paint, and sealer to dry after each application.

1. For table base, use brackets to fasten shutters together from inside.
2. Center tabletop on shutters and glue in place. Use brackets to secure tabletop to base, underneath rim.
3. Following crackle medium manufacturer's instructions and using brown for basecoat and ecru for topcoat, paint table.
4. Apply two to three coats of sealer to table.

SHADOW BOX TABLE

*B*eyond a "shadow" of a doubt, this showcase is sure to become a bedside favorite. A wooden table and lid are sanded and painted, then topped with glass to create a pretty display for your most treasured mementos.

SHADOW BOX TABLE

Recycled items: a small wooden table and a deep wooden lid or picture frame to fit tabletop

You will also need wood glue, sandpaper, tack cloth, light green and black acrylic paint, paintbrushes, paste floor wax, clear acrylic spray sealer, memorabilia items, and a piece of glass to fit tabletop.

Allow glue, paint, and sealer to dry after each application.

1. Glue lid or frame to tabletop.
2. Sand table; wipe with tack cloth. Paint table black. Apply a thin layer of wax to table. Paint table green.
3. Sand table; wipe with tack cloth. Apply two coats of sealer.
4. Arrange items in tabletop. Place glass over table.

OLD-STYLE SETTEE

You'll be sitting pretty on a floral settee made from a refurbished twin-size headboard and footboard. We painted our creation white and brushed it with burnt umber to give it old-fashioned charm.

HEADBOARD SETTEE

Recycled items: twin-size bed foot board and headboard

You will also need a saw, sixteen 2" long corner brackets, drill and bits, four 3" long wood screws, 1" x 4" lumber, white and brown acrylic paint, paintbrush, paste floor wax, sandpaper, tack cloth, $1/2$"-thick plywood, $1/4$"-thick particleboard, $1/2$" long wood screws, 4"-thick foam rubber, fabric for cushion and pillow, staple gun and staples, and an 18" square pillow form.

Allow paint to dry after each application. Use a $1/2$" seam allowance for all sewing unless otherwise indicated.

1. For arms of settee, cut foot board in half.
2. Aligning pieces for desired slant of settee, referring to Fig. 1, and using brackets at inside corners of frame, attach bottom cut end of arm piece to headboard. Drilling a pilot hole first, insert a 3" long screw from back of headboard piece into top cut end of arm piece to secure.

Fig. 1

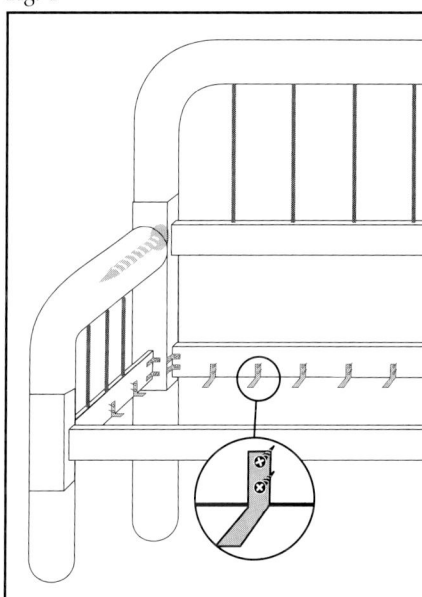

3. For rails, measure and cut a length from 1" x 4" lumber to fit across front of settee between legs and across back between legs. Referring to Step 2, use brackets to attach lumber pieces between legs.
4. Mark center bottom edge on inside of back rail. Working outward from mark, mark edge at 5" intervals. Repeat for each rail. Matching corner of brackets with bottom edge of rails, mount one bracket at each mark.

5. Paint settee white. Lightly brush settee with brown. Apply wax to settee. Repaint settee white. Lightly sand settee, then wipe with tack cloth.
6. Cut a piece of plywood and particleboard to fit in bottom of settee, notch corners if necessary. Place plywood in settee and secure to brackets with $1/2$" long screws.
7. For cushion, cut a piece of foam same size as particleboard, do not notch corners. Cut a piece of fabric 12" larger than foam piece. Place fabric wrong side up on a flat surface. Center foam, then particleboard on fabric. Fold edges of fabric over to particleboard and staple in place. Gather corners and staple to particleboard. Place cushion in settee.
8. Piecing as necessary, cut one 5" x 76" strip from fabric for ruffle. Cut two 19" square pieces from fabric for pillow. Matching right sides, sew short edges of strip together to form a large circle; press seam allowance open. Matching wrong sides and raw edges, press strip in half. Baste along raw edges. Pull basting threads to gather ruffle to fit one pillow square. Matching raw edges, baste ruffle to right side of pillow square.
9. Matching right sides and leaving an opening for turning, pin, then sew pillow squares together. Turn pillow right side out. Insert pillow form in pillow; sew opening closed.

A Refreshing Change

When Baby has outgrown the changing table, "change it" into an attractive bathroom organizer. Scraps of wallpaper line the shelves and the French sign for "The Bath." Painted wicker baskets provide pretty storage space.

BATHROOM ORGANIZER

Recycled items: wooden changing table, two rectangular wicker baskets with wooden bottoms, self-adhesive wallpaper scraps, cardboard, and a small wooden picture frame (we used a 3¼" x 7" frame)

You will also need sandpaper, tack cloth, spray primer, mauve and brown acrylic paint, paintbrushes, glossy wood-tone spray, matte acrylic spray sealer, spray adhesive, hot glue gun, cardstock to coordinate with wallpaper, black permanent medium-point marker, and a saw-tooth hanger.

Allow primer, paint, and sealer to dry after each application. Use spray adhesive for all gluing unless otherwise indicated.

1. Sand table; wipe with tack cloth. Apply primer to table and baskets. Paint table mauve and baskets brown. Apply wood-tone spray, then sealer to table and baskets.
2. For each shelf, measure width and length of inside of shelf and subtract ½" from each measurement; cut one piece of wallpaper the determined measurements. Following manufacturer's instructions, center and smooth wallpaper piece onto shelf.
3. Follow Step 2 to cover inside bottom of each basket with wallpaper.
4. For sign, cut a piece from cardboard and wallpaper to fit in frame. Cover cardboard with wallpaper; hot glue cardboard in frame. Cut a piece from cardstock smaller than frame opening; use marker to write "Le Bain" on cardstock. Using spray adhesive, center and glue cardstock on mat.
5. Attach hanger to back of frame. Hang frame at center back of organizer.

dress up your décor with accessories fashioned from forgotten treasures found at flea markets, yard sales, and discard bins! From bread box to organizer, fan blade to photo screen, teapot to lamp, and more — yesterday's throwaways become distinctive conversation pieces easily created with simple crafting techniques and your own personal touch. These dazzling decorations are as versatile as they are beautiful!

CREATIVE CLOTHESPIN FRAME

Raid your old-fashioned clothespin collection to create our lovely laundry room frame. Showcasing a nostalgic soap advertisement or related print, this accent will make ordinary frames seem all washed up!

CLOTHESPIN FRAME

Recycled items: small flat clothespins, wooden picture frame (we used a 12" x 17" frame), and four buttons

You will also need a drill and bits, craft saw, $1/2$" long decorative nails, hammer, spray primer, ecru acrylic paint, paintbrush, and clear acrylic spray sealer.

Allow primer, paint, and sealer to dry after each application.

1. Refer to Fig. 1 to drill a hole in each clothespin to be nailed to frame.

Fig. 1

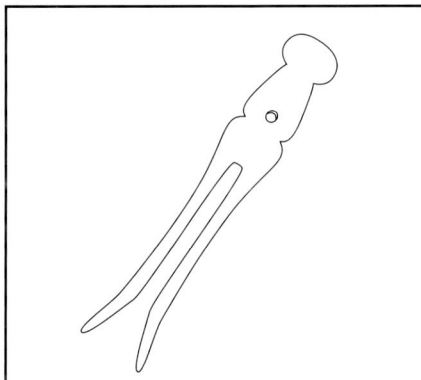

2. For each corner "flower," refer to Fig. 2 to cut one rounded edge from two clothespins and both rounded edges from one clothespin. Arrange clothespins as shown; nail to corner of frame. Nail button to "flower." Attach one flower to each remaining corner of frame.

Fig. 2

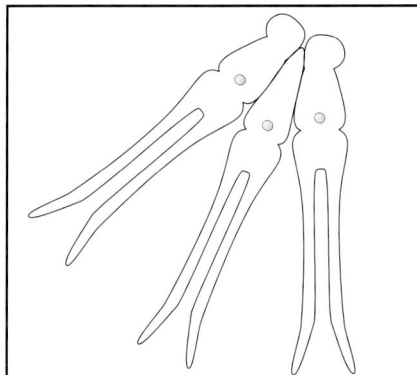

3. Arrange and nail clothespins along edges of frame.

4. Apply primer, then two coats of ecru paint to frame; apply two to three coats of sealer.

APPEALING PLATE RACK

All eyes will be drawn to this appealing plate rack when it graces the walls of your home. Paint some decorative drawer pulls and attach them to a length of lumber to create this nostalgic accent worthy of Grandma's formal dining room.

PLATE RACK

Recycled items: 1" x 6" fence board and decorative double-bolt drawer pulls

You will also need a saw, sandpaper, tack cloth, drill, 2" bolts to fit drawer pulls, white and metallic gold acrylic paint, paintbrushes, decorative wooden trim for top of rack, clear acrylic sealer, $1/4$" dia. clear rubber tubing, hot glue gun, and a heavy-duty saw-tooth picture hanger.

1. Round top end of fence board. Leaving 7" above top plate, spacing plates evenly, and leaving $1^{1}/_{2}$" between plates, arrange desired plates on fence board. Mark board at bottom of each plate and across board 1" below bottom plate; cut board at bottom mark. Sand board, then wipe with tack cloth.
2. Using marks for plates as guides, center and drill holes for drawer pulls on board. Using 2" bolts, attach drawer pulls.
3. Glue trim piece at top of rack. Allowing to dry after each application, paint rack gold, then white; lightly sand for a weathered look. Apply two to three coats of sealer to rack; allow to dry.
4. Cut six pieces from tubing to fit between drawer pull and board. Slit tubes along one side and place over bolts.
5. Attach hanger to back of rack.

"Sew" Fun Notes

Do you have friends who are always on the move? To help you keep in touch, this stationery caddy will be a convenient addition to your home — or a lovely gift for their new abode. It's "sew" simple to make — just paint an old-time sewing machine drawer to have a weathered look.

Stationery Drawer Tote

Recycled item: sewing machine drawer from sewing machine cabinet

You will also need sandpaper, tack cloth, wood glue, four wooden finials for legs, decorative wooden cutout, ivory and brown acrylic paint, paintbrushes, paste floor wax, and clear acrylic spray sealer.

Allow glue, paint, and sealer to dry after each application.

1. Sand drawer; wipe with tack cloth. Glue one leg to each bottom corner of drawer and cutout to front of drawer.
2. Paint drawer brown; apply wax to drawer. Paint drawer ivory, then lightly sand for a weathered look; wipe with tack cloth.
3. Apply two to three coats of sealer to drawer.

CORRUGATED FLOOR LAMP

Add a contemporary look to your living room with this easy-to-make floor lamp. Wood-tone spray enriches the unique corrugated cardboard covers for the weighted coffee-can base and lampshade.

COFFEE CAN FLOOR LAMP

Recycled items: five large coffee cans with plastic lids, lamp with base that will fit in coffee can (we used a 12"h candlestick-type lamp), sand to weight lamp base, and corrugated cardboard

You will also need duct tape, tin snips, hot glue gun, glossy wood-tone and cherry wood-tone spray, and a square lampshade (we used a 5" wide at top, 15" wide at bottom, and 10" high lampshade).

Allow wood-tone spray to dry after each application.

1. For lamp base, fill three coffee cans with sand to weight. Place lids on cans. With weighted cans on bottom, stack and tape four cans together.

2. Cut bottom from remaining can. Use tin snips to cut a notch in bottom of can for lamp cord; hot glue along edges of notch. Center lamp on base; glue to secure. Place can over lamp with cord extending through notch; tape can to base. Tape cord down side of base.

3. For lamp base top, draw around remaining lid on cardboard; cut out. Glue cardboard circle to lid. Cut top from outer edge to center, then trim a hole to fit around lamp. Glue top on base.

4. For lamp base cover, measure height of base. Measure around base. With corrugation running vertically, cut a piece from corrugated paper the determined measurements.

5. Refer to Table to cut and paint pieces of cardboard for checkerboard and lampshade trims. Referring to Diagram, arrange and glue pieces to cover, trimming end piece(s) even with cover as necessary. Wrap and glue cover around base.

6. Center and glue one 3" cherry square and one 1½" square to each side of lampshade. Place lampshade on lamp.

TABLE

#	size	dir.	color
13	3" sq.	||||	cherry
5	3" sq.	≡	wood
12	1½" x 3"	||||	cherry
16	1½" x 3"	≡	wood
4	1½" sq.	||||	cherry

DIAGRAM

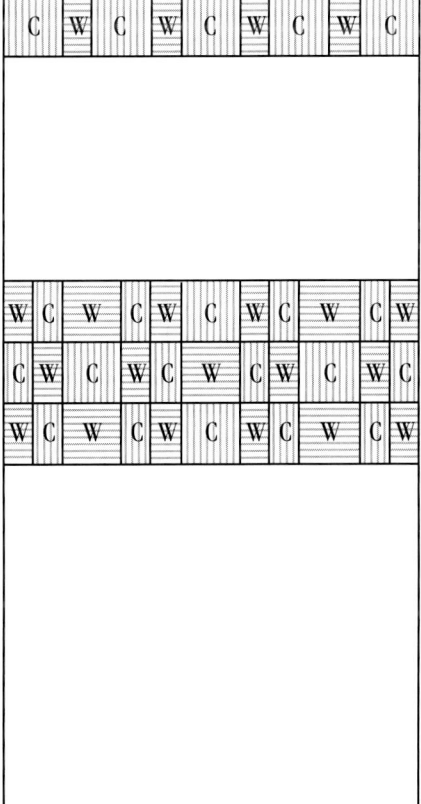

CORK-POPPER'S MESSAGE BOARD

Pop the cork of your creativity and frame a unique arrangement of bottle stoppers for your home! This attractive bulletin board is ideal for posting reminders or telephone messages.

CORK BULLETIN BOARD

Recycled items: wooden picture frame, wine corks, and heavy-weight corrugated cardboard

You will also need sandpaper, tack cloth, primer, tan and brown acrylic paint, paintbrushes, glazing medium, paper towels, hot glue gun, and gimp trim.

Allow paint, primer, and sealer to dry after each application.

1. If necessary, sand frame; wipe with tack cloth. Apply primer, then two coats of tan paint to frame.
2. If necessary, remove glass from frame. Mix one part brown paint with three parts glazing medium. Brush mixture over frame; while still wet, crumple paper towel and pounce on frame randomly to create texture.
3. Trimming to fit, glue trim along opening in frame.
4. Cut a piece of cardboard to fit frame opening; glue cardboard in frame.
5. Trimming to fit, glue corks in opening of frame, covering completely.

MAILBOX WASTEBASKET

Hunt down those annoying piles of junk mail and chunk 'em — into this unique trash can. The metal mailbox is transformed into an ultra-trendy wastebasket with spray paint and an untamed animal print.

MAILBOX TRASH CAN

Recycled item: metal mailbox

You will also need sandpaper, tack cloth, spray primer, orange spray paint, brown and black acrylic paint, paintbrushes, glossy wood-tone spray, and clear acrylic spray sealer.

Allow wood filler, primer, paint, wood-tone spray, and sealer to dry after each application.

1. Remove flag from mailbox. If necessary, sand mailbox to remove rust; wipe with tack cloth.
2. Apply primer, then two coats orange paint to inside and outside of mailbox. Paint brown spots randomly over outside of mailbox; outline spots and paint details black.
3. Apply wood-tone spray, then two to three coats of sealer to trash can.

Perky Lamp

Compliments on your ingenuity will be well-grounded when you show off this remarkable lamp made from parts of an old coffeepot. Use it to perk up after-dinner conversation while waiting for the newer brewer in your kitchen to finish its job!

PERCOLATOR LAMP

Recycled items: basket, basket lid, and stem from percolator coffeepot

You will also need gold acrylic paint, paintbrushes, three 1" dia. wooden beads, clear acrylic sealer, hot glue gun, three $1/2$" long sheet metal screws, two 1" dia. check rings, welding compound, gravel, large (dome-head) and small (flat head) upholstery nails, $3/4$" x $1/2$" IP threaded pipe nipple, one $1/2$" dia. flat locknut, socket shell and base, electrical cord for wiring lamp, aluminum foil, lampshade to fit lamp, rolling pin, craft glue, soft cloth, $3/8$"w gold mesh ribbon, and a pair of wire cutters.

Use hot glue for all gluing unless otherwise indicated. Allow paint, sealer, welding compound, and craft glue to dry after each application. Refer to Diagram to assemble lamp.

1. For feet, paint beads gold; apply two to three coats of sealer.
2. Glue beads to top of lid (as lid would fit on basket), then use sheet metal screws to secure.
3. Place one check ring on stem, then place stem through basket. Follow manufacturer's instructions to "weld" stem to bottom of basket. Fill basket with gravel. "Weld" lid to basket. Turn basket upside down for lamp base.
4. Hammer large nails evenly along top of basket. Hammer small nails 1" apart on sides of base near bottom.
5. "Weld" threaded pipe at top of stem. Thread remaining check ring and locknut on threaded pipe. Twist socket base onto threaded pipe.
6. Thread electrical cord from bottom to top through stem. Loosen screws on socket shell. Wrap wires from one strand of cord around one screw twice; tighten screw. Repeat for remaining wires and screw. Snap socket shell into socket base.
7. Cut a piece from foil large enough to cover lampshade. Lightly crumple foil, then smooth out. Place foil on a flat surface; use rolling pin to flatten foil.
8. Using craft glue, wrap and glue foil around lampshade. Fold edges of foil to inside top and bottom of shade and hot glue in place.
9. Working in small sections, apply gold paint to lampshade, then wipe immediately with a soft cloth for a "tarnished" look.
10. Trimming to fit, use craft glue to glue ribbon around top and bottom of shade.
11. Spacing evenly, push small nails through ribbon around shade; use wire cutters to cut off points on inside of shade. Apply hot glue to cut ends of nails.

DIAGRAM

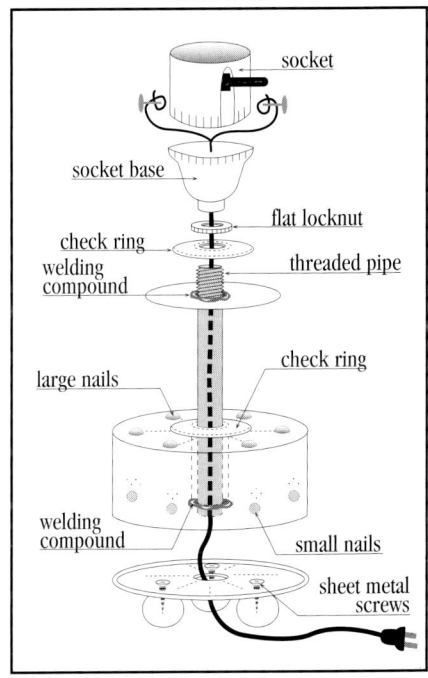

BELTED FOOTSTOOL

When you come home from a hard day at the office, take a load off by propping your feet up on this comfy footstool. It's easy to fashion from an old leather coat and belt in no time.

BELTED FOOTSTOOL

Recycled items: wooden footstool, leather coat, and a leather belt (to fit and buckle around stool)

You will also need 4" thick foam, muslin, hot glue gun, staple gun, plain and decorative upholstery tacks, and a hammer.

1. Draw around top of stool on foam, muslin, and wrong side of leather coat. Cut out foam along drawn line; cut out muslin and leather 1½" outside drawn lines.

2. Glue foam shape to top of stool. Cut sharp edges from top of foam shape.

3. Stretch muslin piece over foam, stapling muslin to edge of stool. Stretch leather piece over muslin, using plain tacks to secure leather to edge of stool.

4. Buckle belt around edge of stool; glue end of belt in place at buckle. Use decorative tacks to secure belt in place.

"KEY TO MY HEART" FRAME

There's no need for Cupid's help in winning over that special someone when you can make this sentimental gift. With its message of "You hold the key to my Heart" repeated on the antique-looking background, the classy doorknob and keys will open the door to anyone's soul.

KEY TO MY HEART FRAME

Recycled items: three skeleton keys, brass charm, key plate, wooden picture frame, and a doorknob

You will also need parchment tissue paper, stretched canvas to fit in frame, black permanent fine-point marker, decoupage glue, foam paintbrushes, crackle medium, clear acrylic brush-on sealer, antique gold antiquing medium, soft cloth, brown metal paint, paintbrushes, gold acrylic paint, craft glue, craft knife and cutting mat, bolt and washer to attach doorknob, $1/16$" wide and $3/8$" wide ribbons, and a hot glue gun.

Allow decoupage glue, sealer, antiquing medium, paint, and craft glue to dry after each application. Use craft glue for all gluing unless otherwise indicated.

1. Cut a piece from tissue paper 2" larger than canvas. Spacing lines approximately 1" apart, use marker to write "You hold the key to my Heart"; repeat to cover tissue paper. Use decoupage glue to attach tissue paper to canvas. Follow manufacturer's instructions to apply crackle medium, sealer, then antiquing medium to canvas over tissue.

2. Paint keys, charm, key plate, and frame brown. Use finger to lightly apply gold paint to keys, charm, key plate, and frame as desired.

3. Center key plate on canvas; glue in place. Use craft knife to cut a small "X" in canvas at hole in key plate for doorknob; use bolt and washer to attach doorknob.

4. Thread keys onto $1/16$" wide ribbon, then knot ends together; repeat for charm. Tie $3/8$" wide ribbon into a bow. Arrange keys, charm, and bow on canvas; glue in place.

5. Place canvas in frame; hot glue to secure.

PICTURE-PERFECT SOFTWARE

Finally, computer software that can handle multiple applications! This useful cover, constructed from a vinyl tablecloth and fabric scraps, will protect your monitor from dust while providing a pleasing gallery for your favorite snapshots.

COMPUTER MONITOR COVER

Recycled items: flannel-backed vinyl tablecloth

You will also need kraft paper, clear tape, clear vinyl, extra wide double fold bias tape, and fabric glue.

1. For pattern, measure height of monitor from front top corner to table; add $1/2$". Measure width across front of monitor; add $1/2$". Cut a piece of kraft paper the determined measurements. Repeat for back of monitor.
2. Using measurements determined in Step 1, multiply front height measurement by 2; add front width measurement. Measure depth of monitor, front to back; add $1/2$". Cut a piece of paper the determined measurements.
3. Matching side edges, fold each paper piece in half. Aligning folds and edges of paper, refer to Diagram to tape pieces together. Using back height measurement determined in Step 1 and measuring outward from side edges of back paper piece, mark back edge of center paper piece. Draw a line from front corner of center paper piece to mark on each side of pattern; cut along drawn lines.
4. Pin pattern on right side of tablecloth; cut out along pattern edges. Remove pattern.
5. For portrait photo pockets, cut a strip of clear vinyl $6^{1}/_{2}$"w by the front width measurement determined in Step 1.
6. For landscape photo pockets, cut a strip of clear vinyl $4^{1}/_{2}$"w by the front width measurement determined in Step 1.
7. Arrange strips across cover front and tape in place. Leaving top edge open and using a $1/4$" seam allowance, sew along bottom and sides of strips. Remove tape. Adding $1/4$" to width of each photo, mark pockets on strips; sew along marks.
8. Matching wrong sides and referring to Fig.1 to match edges, use a $1/4$" seam allowance to sew corner edges together. Sew a $1/4$" seam along front and back top edges.
9. Beginning at one bottom front corner and trimming ends even with bottom edges of cover, glue seam allowance along front edges in fold of bias tape. Repeat for back of cover.

DIAGRAM

NOTABLE CD HOLDER

Friends can't help but take note of your favorite music groups when you rack up your CDs in this decorative box. Music-motif fabric and felt cutouts put a new spin on discarded shoeboxes.

SHOEBOX CD HOLDER

Recycled item: child-size angle-edge shoeboxes

You will also need a hot glue gun, fabric, spray adhesive, felt, tracing paper, black acrylic paint, paintbrush, and four $1\frac{1}{4}$" dia. wooden ball-shaped knobs.

1. Hot glue tall ends of boxes together. Draw around box on wrong side of fabric. Measure height of box at center; multiply by 2 and add $\frac{1}{2}$". Mark fabric outside lines the determined height; cut out.
2. Refer to Diagram to cut away corners of fabric along dotted lines. Apply spray adhesive to wrong side of fabric. Reposition box on fabric. Overlapping to inside edges, smooth long edges, then short edges onto box.
3. Cut a piece of fabric to cover divider. Apply spray adhesive to wrong side of fabric; smooth piece over divider.
4. Cut pieces of felt to cover inside bottoms of box sections. Apply spray adhesive to one side of each piece; smooth in place.
5. Trace note pattern, page 146, onto tracing paper; cut three music notes from felt. Use spray adhesive to glue notes to box.
6. For feet, paint knobs black; allow to dry. Hot glue feet to bottom of box.

DIAGRAM

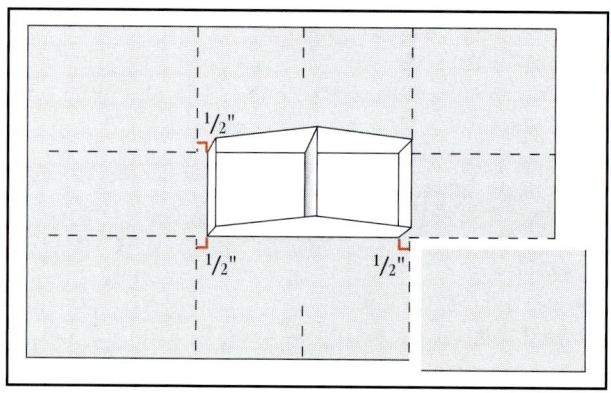

Time in the Balance

Don't let today's fast-paced lifestyle blur your sense of what's important in life. Made from a kitchen scale, this unique decorator clock will remind you to weigh your priorities each time you look at it.

SCALE CLOCK

Recycled items: top-weighing scale, lightweight cardboard, and a scrap of wallpaper

You will also need spray adhesive, hammer, awl, battery-operated clock kit, spray primer, desired color for basecoat and brown acrylic paint, paintbrushes, soft cloth, clear acrylic spray sealer, and craft glue.

Allow primer, paint, sealer, and glue to dry after each application.

1. Remove ring and dial plate from scale; set ring aside. Using dial plate as a pattern, cut one piece each from cardboard and wallpaper for clock face.
2. Apply spray adhesive to wrong side of wallpaper piece and smooth onto cardboard piece. Use hammer and awl to make a hole at center of clock face. Follow manufacturer's instructions to assemble clock using clock face.
3. Apply primer to scale; paint scale desired color.
4. Make a wash using one part brown paint and two parts water. Working in small sections, apply wash to scale and wipe area immediately with soft cloth. Apply two to three coats of sealer to scale.
5. Glue clock face in ring; replace ring on scale.

DAPPER DRAWER OTTOMAN

Guests will never guess that this dapper ottoman once was a chest drawer. Topped with a hinged, padded lid, the slyly disguised footrest stands on classic turned wooden legs. The inside is nicely lined for storing afghans and other comforts.

DRAWER OTTOMAN

Recycled items: drawer from chest of drawers and heavy-weight corrugated cardboard

You will also need a saw, 1/2" plywood, 1" flat-head wood screws, batting, fabric, staple gun, lining fabric, wood glue, hot glue gun, 1/2"w gimp braid, 1"-thick foam, hinge the length of one long edge of drawer, four leg mount brackets, spray primer, desired colors of acrylic paint for basecoat and top coat on legs, paintbrushes, paste floor wax, sandpaper, tack cloth, clear acrylic spray sealer, and braided fringe.

Drill a pilot hole before driving screws into wood. Use wood glue for all gluing unless otherwise indicated. Allow wood glue, primer, and paint to dry after each application.

1. Remove hardware from drawer. If necessary, use a saw to carefully trim drawer front edges even with sides, top, and bottom of drawer.
2. Draw around drawer two times on plywood; cut out pieces along drawn lines. Use screws to attach one piece of plywood to bottom of drawer.
3. Measure height of drawer; add 5". Measure around drawer; add 1". Cut pieces of batting and fabric the determined measurements. Centering batting on front of drawer, wrap ends to back; staple in place.
4. Press one short edge of fabric $1/2$" to wrong side. Beginning with pressed edge at one back corner and 1" of fabric extending past bottom edge of drawer, wrap fabric around drawer; overlap pressed edge over raw edge at corner. Fold extra fabric to bottom and inside of drawer; staple on bottom and inside to secure.
5. Measure height and width of inside sides and bottom of drawer. Use the determined measurements to cut two bottom, two end, and two side pieces from cardboard. Cut pieces of lining fabric 2" larger on each side than each cardboard piece. Center each cardboard piece on wrong side of corresponding lining piece; fold lining corners diagonally to back of cardboard and glue to secure. Pulling fabric taut, glue fabric edges to back of cardboard. Use wood glue to glue pieces over insides of drawer, lining side out. Set remaining bottom piece aside.
6. Hot glue gimp over edges of lining along top of drawer.
7. For lid, draw around remaining plywood piece on foam, batting, and fabric. Cut out foam along dawn lines and batting and fabric 4" outside drawn lines. Center batting, foam, then plywood on wrong side of fabric. Folding at corners and pulling fabric taut, fold edges over to plywood and staple in place. Staple remaining bottom lining piece to bottom of lid. Glue gimp over edges of lining.
8. Following manufacturer's instructions, use hinge to attach lid to back edge of drawer. Attach one leg mount at each corner on bottom of drawer.
9. Paint legs with primer, then basecoat color. Apply wax along edges of legs. Paint legs top coat color. Lightly sand legs along edges; wipe with tack cloth. Apply two coats of sealer to legs. Attach legs to leg brackets.
10. Overlapping ends at one back corner, hot glue fringe along bottom of drawer.

OLD-FASHIONED FLAIR

Beautiful glass doorknobs from an old house or the flea market can add flair to your walls. Mounted on a painted plaque, the dainty knobs make a useful adornment for any room.

DOORKNOB HANGING RACK

Recycled items: three glass doorknobs with shafts removed

You will also need a wooden plaque large enough to accommodate doorknobs, drill and bits, white and green acrylic paint, paintbrushes, three $1\frac{1}{2}$" long bolts to fit in holes of doorknobs, craft glue, and a saw-tooth picture hanger.

1. Arrange doorknobs on plaque to mark placement for drilling holes; drill holes in plaque.

2. Paint plaque green; allow to dry. *Dry Brush,* page 158, plaque white; allow to dry.

3. Working from back to front, push bolts through holes. Apply glue to bolts; twist doorknobs onto bolts.

4. Attach hanger to top back of plaque.

GRAPEVINE NOTEBOX

Hear the latest news on the grapevine. Family members will love this grape-embellished message holder, fashioned from a metal city mailbox with a lock flap and lid.

DESIGNER MAILBOX

Recycled item: metal wall-mount mailbox with lock flap and flap lid

You will also need sandpaper; tack cloth; spray primer; ecru spray paint; white, yellow, light purple, purple, dark purple, light green, green, and dark green acrylic paint; flat, liner, and assorted paintbrushes; black paint pen; and clear acrylic spray sealer.

Refer to Painting Techniques, page 157, before beginning project. Allow primer, paint, and sealer to dry after each application.

1. If necessary, sand mailbox to remove rust; wipe with tack cloth.
2. Apply primer, then two coats of ecru paint to mailbox. Paint lock flap yellow and lid flap green. Use paint pen to write "Notes" on flap.
3. Use fingertip to apply dark purple, purple, and light purple dots in bunches for grapes; add white highlights to a few grapes.
4. Paint leaves, tendrils, and dots around leaves and grapes as desired.
5. Apply two to three coats of sealer to mailbox.

GAS CAN LAMP

*P*ut an interesting twist on traditional lighting by creating a quaint lamp from a weather-beaten petrol can. Add a fabric-covered lampshade with button tabs for a result that's sure to fuel your decorative fire!

GAS CAN LAMP

Recycled items: metal gas can and seven $3/4$" dia. buttons

You will also need a jar lamp kit, wooden plate larger than bottom of can, black acrylic paint, paintbrush, household cement, drill with $3/8$" bit, sand, lampshade, fabric, craft glue, and $1/2$"w single fold bias tape.

Use craft glue for all gluing unless otherwise indicated. Allow paint, household cement, and craft glue to dry after each application.

1. Wash can with soap and water until no fumes remain; rinse thoroughly and allow to dry.
2. Paint plate black. Use household cement to glue bottom of can to bottom of plate.
3. Remove lid from can. Drill a hole at center of lid. Remove and discard lid from lamp kit. Follow manufacturer's instructions to assemble lamp on can lid. Fill can with sand. Replace lid on can.
4. For lampshade cover, measure around bottom of lampshade; multiply by $1^1/2$. Measure height of lampshade; add $1^1/2$". Cut a piece from fabric using the determined measurements. Matching right sides, glue short edges together to form a tube. Turn cover right side out. Baste along raw edges of cover.
5. Place cover over lampshade. Pull basting threads to gather top and bottom edges of cover to fit lampshade; knot ends together and trim thread ends. Folding raw edges to inside of lampshade and spacing gathers evenly, glue ends of cover to inside top and bottom of lampshade. Trimming to fit, glue bias tape over raw edges inside top of lampshade.
6. Measure around bottom of lampshade; add $1/2$". Cut a strip from fabric 8"w by the determined measurement. Matching right sides, use a $1/4$" seam allowance to sew short edges together; turn right side out. Glue right side of one raw edge of strip along inside bottom rim of lampshade.
7. Cut six $3^1/2$" long pieces of bias tape for tabs; press one end of each tab $1/2$" to wrong side. Spacing evenly around lampshade, glue unpressed end of each tab to inside bottom rim of lampshade. Gathering fabric strip at each tab, fold and glue pressed end of tab to front. Glue one button over end of each tab.

Sensational Serving Tray

*Y*our plate will be full of compliments when you stack up some goodies on this three-tier tray. Delicate crystal candleholders and glass plates glued together create this sensational server.

THREE-TIER SERVER

Recycled items: three clear glass plates (we used 11", 9", and 8" dia. plates) and two clear glass candleholders

You will also need clear-drying household cement.

Allow cement to dry after each application.

1. Wash plates and candleholders in warm soapy water; allow to dry.
2. With largest plate on bottom, use cement to glue plates and candleholders together to form server; allow to dry.

BATHING BEAUTIES

Filled with fragrant oils, these bathing beauties will enrich any bathroom. Simply top off assorted bottles with fancy lightbulbs, sponge-paint in jewel tones, and swirl with wire.

BATH OIL BOTTLES

Recycled items: assorted bottles with openings large enough to accommodate corks and small-base lightbulbs

You will also need rubbing alcohol, cotton balls, natural sponge pieces, desired colors of glass paint, clear acrylic spray sealer, corks to fit bottle opening, and soldering wire.

Refer to Painting Techniques, page 157, before beginning project.

1. Clean bottles and bulbs with alcohol. *Sponge Paint* each bottle and lightbulb; while paint is still wet, add *Marbleizing* details as desired. Apply two to three coats of sealer to bottle and lightbulb; allow to dry.
2. Place cork in bottle. Make a hole in cork slightly smaller than base of lightbulb; twist lightbulb into hole.
3. Carefully wrap and curl wire around bottle and lightbulb as desired.

MOSAIC MASTERPIECE

This mosaic is everything it's cracked up to be — a lovely work of art that will elicit lots of compliments. Instead of expensive tile or ceramic scraps, we used bleached and painted eggshells to form the simple floral design.

EGGSHELL MOSAIC

Recycled items: about 20 eggshell halves, wooden picture frame with $2^{1}/_{2}$" x $4^{1}/_{2}$" opening, and cardboard

You will also need rubber gloves; chlorine bleach; clear jar; paper towels; white, yellow, pink, blue, purple, green, and black acrylic paint; paintbrushes; tracing paper; transfer paper; craft glue; and clear acrylic spray sealer.

Allow paint, glue, and sealer to dry after each application.

1. (*Caution:* Wear rubber gloves and work in a well-ventilated area when working with bleach.) Thoroughly rinse eggshells in water. Place eggshells in a jar and cover with one part bleach to one part water. Place lid on jar and allow eggshells to soak 24 hours. Remove eggshells from jar and place on several layers of paper towels to dry.

2. Draw around opening of frame on cardboard; cut out $^{1}/_{2}$" outside drawn line. Paint one side of cardboard black.

3. Trace flower design, page 155, onto tracing paper. Use transfer paper to transfer design to center of black side of cardboard; draw border $^{1}/_{2}$" inside edges.

4. Painting both sides of shells, paint six eggshell halves green, two each yellow, pink, blue, and purple. Leave remaining eggshells unpainted.

5. Keeping colors separate, break eggshells into small pieces. Using glue to secure, arrange eggshell pieces over design; use unpainted eggshell pieces to fill in background to border lines.

6. Lightly apply wax to frame. Paint frame white, then use finger to lightly apply green and pink paint to frame. Use soft cloth to wipe paint from waxed areas.

7. Glue design in frame. Apply two to three coats of sealer to frame and design.

FLASHY PHOTO TREE

Capture the mood of decades past with this flashy photo tree. Family pictures from long ago bring memories to life when displayed on an array of twisted wires anchored by a vintage camera.

CAMERA PHOTO TREE

Recycled items: camera (we used a Brownie Hawkeye® with flash attachment) and photographs

You will also need 18-gauge wire, wire cutters, ruler, pliers, and a hot glue gun.

1. Cut five 15" lengths of wire. Using pliers, bend one end of each wire into a squared coil to hold photos.
2. Place straight ends of wires together; twist 2" of wires together to secure.
3. Glue twisted wire ends to camera. Arrange wires, then photographs in coils.

BEADED BEDAZZLERS

It's easy to transform empty food jars into jazzy candleholders! Simply thread beads onto wire and then twist and swirl into random shapes that strike your fancy.

BEADED JARS

Recycled items: assorted glass jars

You will also need 20-gauge black craft wire, wire cutters, needle-nose pliers, and beads in assorted shapes and sizes.

1. For each jar, cut a 26" length of wire. Coil beginning end of wire in a ½" dia. circle. Making bends in wire as desired, wrap wire around jar.

2. Remove wire and thread beads along bends; coil remaining end of wire, cutting excess wire if necessary. Place wire around jar; wrap beginning coiled end through bend in wire to secure.

3. If an additional drop is desired, bend one end of a short piece of wire into a loop. Thread desired beads onto wire and coil end to secure. Thread loop onto bottom coil of first wire.

Cookbook Stand

Take a stand for kitchen efficiency with this handy helper! To craft a proper prop for cookbooks, mix together an easel-backed, wooden picture frame, themed wrapping paper, and hand-painted dollhouse molding.

BOOK STAND

Recycled items: wooden picture frame with easel frame back and wrapping paper

You will also need spray adhesive, craft saw, desired colors of acrylic paint, paintbrushes, dollhouse molding, small wood screws, craft glue, and clear acrylic spray sealer.

Allow paint, sealer, and glue to dry after each application.

1. Draw around frame back on wrong side of wrapping paper; cut out. Apply spray adhesive to wrong side of paper; smooth paper onto front of frame back.
2. For book rest, use saw to cut a piece of the frame to fit across bottom of stand.
3. Paint dollhouse molding piece and book rest desired color.
4. Working from back of stand, use screws to attach frame back to book rest. (Fig. 1).

Fig. 1

5. Cut dollhouse molding to fit sides and top of stand; glue in place. Paint cut ends of molding. Paint *Comma Strokes and Dots*, page 157, along edges. Apply sealer to stand.

DECOUPAGED BIRD PLAQUES

A pair of bird-embellished plaques will add harmony to a room's décor. To create this lovely look, decoupage images from your favorite greeting cards onto castoff burner covers or the lids of tin canisters.

BIRD PLAQUES

Recycled items: metal burner covers or tin canister lids and greeting cards

You will also need sandpaper (optional), tack cloth (optional), spray primer, white and green acrylic paint, paintbrush, soft cloth, and decoupage glue.

Allow primer, paint, and glue to dry after each application.

1. If necessary, sand covers to remove rust; wipe with tack cloth.
2. Apply primer, then two coats of green paint to burner covers. For wash, mix two parts white paint with one part water. Apply wash to burner covers and wipe off with a soft cloth.
3. Follow *Decoupage*, page 157, to apply motifs from greeting cards to plaques.

"Fan" Club Photo Screen

Show family members and friends that you're a big fan by displaying their pictures for all to see. Make this one-of-a-kind accessory by joining ceiling fan blades and applying a distressed painting technique. The gilded frames are cut from corrugated cardboard.

Fan Blade Photo Display

Recycled items: four wooden ceiling fan blades (with hardware removed) and corrugated cardboard

You will also need a saw, wood filler, drill and 1/8" drill bit, spray primer, crackle medium, ecru and gold acrylic paint, paintbrushes, clear acrylic sealer, tissue paper, cutting mat, craft knife, craft glue, craft sticks, soft cloth, hot glue gun, and 1/16" dia. gold cord.

Use craft glue for all gluing unless otherwise indicated. Allow wood filler, primer, paint, sealer, and craft glue to dry after each application.

1. Measuring from rounded end, cut fan blades to 19" tall. If necessary, fill mounting holes with wood filler. Refer to Fig. 1 to drill holes in blades 1/2" from edges.

Fig. 1

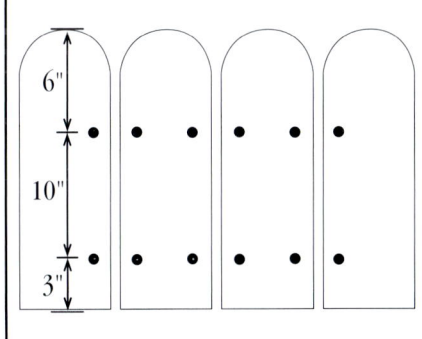

2. Apply primer to blades. Following crackle medium manufacturer's instructions and using gold for basecoat and ecru for topcoat, paint blades.
3. Apply two to three coats of sealer to blades.
4. For each photo frame, cut a 4" square from cardboard. Cut a 2 3/8" square from center of 4" square.
5. Lightly crumple a 5" square of tissue paper, then smooth out. Place tissue paper square on cutting mat; center cardboard square on tissue paper. Cutting tissue paper from corner to corner, cut an "X" in center of opening. Glue tissue paper to front of frame; trimming as necessary, fold and glue center portion to back of frame.
6. Cut three 3" long pieces from craft sticks; glue along sides and bottom of frame back.
7. Working in small sections, paint frame gold and wipe immediately with a soft cloth.
8. Gluing along craft sticks, hot glue frames on blades. Use cord to lace blades together.

Chef's Gadget Lamp

Mix up a handy kitchen lamp for your favorite cook, using the tools of her trade. A metal colander, flour sifter, and measuring spoons are the main ingredients needed to whip up this novel recipe.

KITCHEN LAMP

Recycled items: 5-cup flour sifter, metal colander, and metal measuring spoons

You will also need a drill and bits; ³⁄₈" dia. rubber grommet; foam core board; drawing compass; craft knife and cutting mat; clear silicone sealer; lamp kit with 10" threaded pipe; plaster of paris; craft stick; sandpaper; tack cloth; 4" long plastic candelabra sleeve; clip-on adapter for lampshade; silver spray paint; 24-gauge wire; wire cutters; and a standard-base lightbulb.

Use silicone sealer for all gluing unless otherwise indicated. Allow sealer to dry after each application. Refer to Diagram to assemble lamp.

1. Remove all inner parts of sifter (except hand crank and shaft if applicable); discard. Drill a $3/8$" dia. hole just above bottom rim for cord to pass through. Insert grommet in hole.
2. Draw around bottom of sifter on foam core board; cut out circle just inside drawn line. Use compass to draw a $3/8$" dia. circle at center of foam core circle; cut out. Place circle into sifter 1" from bottom; glue along edges above and below circle to secure.
3. Place threaded pipe into sifter through hole in circle; bend shaft slightly to accommodate threaded pipe. Twist locknut onto pipe under circle until even with end of pipe. Twist remaining locknut onto pipe inside sifter until snug against foam core circle.
4. Follow manufacturer's instructions to mix enough plaster to fill sifter to 1" below lowest part of top rim. Hold pipe at center until plaster sets around it; as plaster sets, use craft stick to gently add texture to top of plaster, to resemble flour.
5. Measure pipe from top of plaster to top of pipe and subtract $3/8$"; cut candelabra sleeve the determined measurement. Place sleeve on pipe.
6. Thread electrical cord through grommet and up pipe to top of lamp. Follow manufacturer's instructions to wire lamp.
7. Drill a hole at center of colander for top of clip-on adapter to fit through; drill small holes 2" apart around rim of colander.
8. If necessary, sand colander and spoons to remove rust; wipe with tack cloth. Paint colander and spoons silver; allow to dry.
9. Use pieces of wire to attach spoons to colander through holes around rim. Attach adapter to colander. Place lightbulb in light socket, then shade on lamp; secure with finial.

DIAGRAM

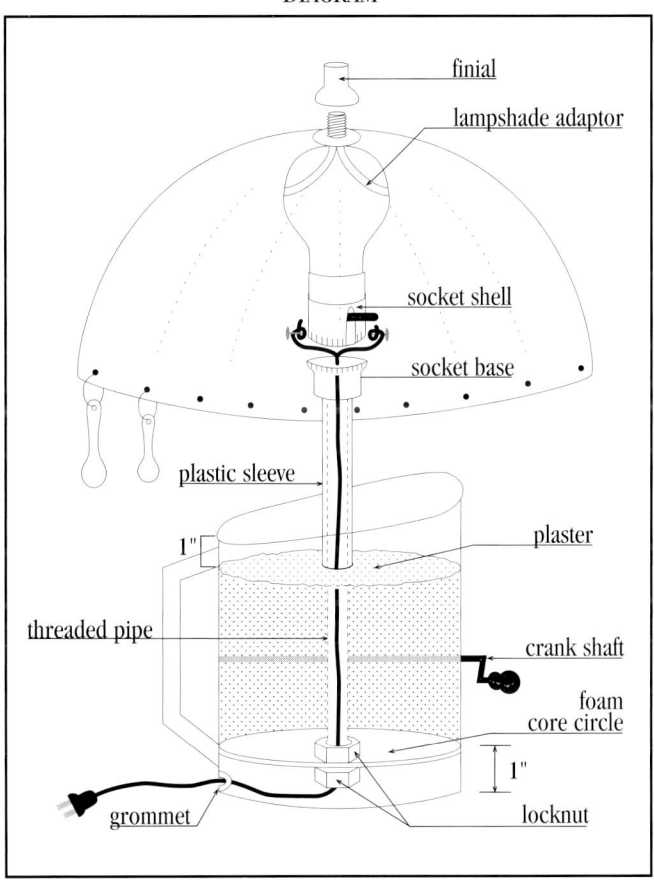

DISTINCTIVE MESSAGES

Bored with a plain-looking message center? Dress it up with a distinctive memo board — constructed from a rescued wooden picture frame. A gold buffing compound gives this masterpiece its gilded finish.

FRAMED CORKBOARD

Recycled items: decorative wooden picture frame and heavy-weight cardboard

You will also need sandpaper, tack cloth, spray primer, brown and dark brown acrylic paint, paintbrushes, soft cloth, metallic gold wax rub-on finish, roll cork, spray adhesive, and a hot glue gun.

Allow primer and paint to dry after each application.

1. Sand frame, then wipe with tack cloth.
2. Apply primer, then two coats brown paint to frame. For wash, mix one part dark brown paint with two parts water. Working in small sections, apply wash to frame and wipe immediately with soft cloth.
3. Follow manufacturer's instructions to apply rub-on finish to frame.
4. For corkboard, cut a piece of cardboard and cork to fit in frame opening. Use spray adhesive to attach cork to cardboard. Hot glue corkboard into frame.

GLOBAL LAMP

An illuminating item for any globe-trotter, this lamp is "home-spun." Gold acrylic paint and cording add the elegant touch you need to bring a world of light into your home or office.

GLOBE LAMPSHADE

Recycled items: a cardboard globe

You will also need a saw, gold acrylic paint, paintbrush, hot glue gun, gold cord, and lampshade adapter.

1. For shade, cut globe in half along the equator. Paint inside of shade gold; allow to dry.
2. Trimming as necessary, glue cord around bottom of shade.
3. Follow manufacturer's instructions to attach lampshade adapter through axis hole in top of globe shade.
4. Place shade on lamp.

POSTAL POCKETS

*F*orget messy mail stacks cluttering your entry hall table. You can create an elegant and convenient place to sort the mail for each family member. Just attach pretty plastic pockets to a paper-covered cardboard base.

MAIL HOLDER

Recycled items: cardboard fabric bolt and three plastic 2-liter bottles

You will also need handmade paper, craft glue, foam brush, jute twine, hot glue gun, decorative tissue paper, stapler, corrugated craft cardboard, craft knife, cutting mat, and a 1" dia. metal grommet.

1. Tear handmade paper into large pieces. Mix two parts craft glue with one part water. Using foam brush to apply glue mixture to wrong sides of paper pieces and overlapping edges, glue paper pieces over entire bolt; allow to dry.

2. Spacing jute $3^{1}/_{4}$" apart and knotting ends at back, wrap two pieces of jute lengthwise around bolt.

3. For each pocket, cut a 5" ring from center of bottle (Fig. 1). Lightly crumple tissue paper; smooth out. Use foam brush to apply glue mixture to inside and outside of ring; smooth tissue paper onto ring and allow to dry.

Fig. 1

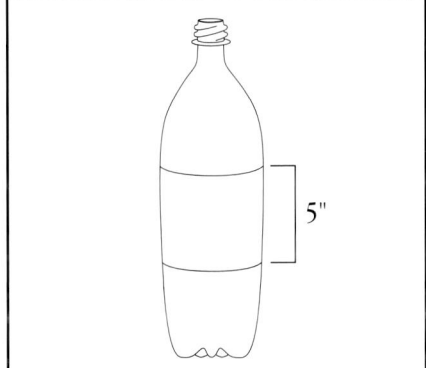

4. For bottom of each pocket, staple one end of pocket closed. Measure width of bottom of pocket. Cut one $1^{1}/_{2}$"w strip from cardboard the determined measurement. Matching smooth sides and long edges, fold cardboard in half. Hot glue bottom of pocket between folds of cardboard.

5. Arrange and hot glue pockets on front of bolt.

6. For hanger, use craft knife to make a hole at top back center of bolt to fit grommet, hot glue grommet in hole.

HOT NEWS BOARD

*C*ook up a message center with fresh-from-the-oven appeal using a discarded cookie sheet, chalkboard spray paint, and novelty magnets. It's ideal for posting the day's hottest news in the kitchen or a child's room.

COOKIE SHEET MEMO HOLDER

Recycled items: steel cookie sheet, a domino, magnetic letters, and other assorted small toys and game pieces

You will also need sandpaper, tack cloth, spray primer, black chalkboard spray paint, flat paintbrush, red acrylic paint, hot glue gun, magnet dots, and a self-adhesive picture hanger.

Allow primer and paint to dry after each application.

1. If necessary, sand cookie sheet to remove rust; wipe with tack cloth.
2. Spray cookie sheet with primer, then black paint.
3. Use paintbrush and red paint to create checkerboard pattern along edges of cookie sheet. 
4. Glue domino along bottom edge of cookie sheet for chalk holder. Glue letters across top of memo holder and magnets to back of toys.
5. Attach hanger to top back of memo holder.

LADYBUG TRICYCLE

*Y*our li'l peddler will go "buggy" over this striking tyke trike. Yellow and green spray paint provide the vibrant background for the playful ladybug pattern.

PAINTED TRICYCLE

Recycled item: metal tricycle

You will also need sandpaper, tack cloth, spray primer; yellow, red, and green spray paint; red and black metal paint; paintbrushes; and clear acrylic spray sealer.

Allow primer, paint, and sealer to dry after each application. More than one coat of paint may be necessary for desired coverage.

1. Disassemble tricycle. If necessary, sand frame, seat, and footrest to remove rust; wipe with tack cloth.
2. Apply primer to frame, seat, and footrest. Spray paint frame yellow, seat red, and footrest green.
3. Use red metal paint to paint red ladybug bodies on frame. Use black metal paint to paint heads, dots, and detail lines on ladybugs. Paint a ladybug head, dots, and wing detail lines on seat.
4. Apply two to three coats of sealer to painted areas.
5. Reassemble tricycle.

Cozy Cabin

Step back to the days of the pioneers with this cozy lighted cabin! Crafted from a discarded box, the tiny dwelling is reinforced with cardboard-strip "logs" that are dry-brushed for a wood-grain effect. The pebbled chimney is constructed using a candy box and a small bottle.

LIGHTED CABIN

Recycled items: corrugated cardboard, lightweight brown paper bag, and a paper towel tube

You will also need a utility knife; cutting mat; craft glue; hot glue gun; beige, tan, and brown acrylic paint; paintbrushes; sand; foam brushes; medium-weight craft steel; utility scissors; aquarium gravel; a 4-watt electrical wiring harness with socket clip; and a 4-watt cool-burning bulb.

Use craft glue for all gluing unless otherwise indicated. Allow craft glue and paint to dry after each application.

1. Cut a $13^1/2$" x $25^1/2$" piece from cardboard. Referring to Diagram, page 155, mark red and blue guidelines, then cabin sections (black lines), on cardboard piece; cut out cabin along solid black lines. Lightly score cardboard along dashed lines (outside of cabin). Cut out windows, door, and light hole.
2. Glue pieces of paper bag over windows and door on inside of cardboard piece. Fold cardboard to shape cabin; hot glue tabs to inside to secure.
3. Mix one part beige paint with one part sand. Leaving gables unpainted, use foam brush to apply paint mixture to cabin. For "logs," cut several $3/4$"w strips from cardboard. Trimming to fit, glue strips around cabin. Using brown paint, *Dry Brush*, page 158, strips and gables.
4. For roof, cut an $8^1/8$" square from craft steel. Follow manufacturer's instructions to "rust" roof. Glue roof to cabin.
5. For chimney, cut paper towel tube to 8". Cut a 4" slit down one side of tube. Overlap cut edges 1" and hot glue to secure. With overlap at side, pinch end to "square" top of chimney; shape bottom end into an oval. Paint inside top of chimney brown. Paint outside of chimney tan. Glue overlapped side of chimney to end of house.
6. To "rock" chimney, mix one part tan paint with two parts craft glue. Working with one small section at a time, use foam brush to apply paint and glue mixture to chimney; press gravel into mixture.
7. Insert light into back of cabin.

CORRUGATED FRAMES

Memories preserved with flair are memories that will always be there! Framed by the simplistic look of corrugated cardboard, pictures of pleasant times in the past will remind you of precious blessings in the present.

CORRUGATED CARDBOARD FRAMES

Recycled items: photographs, cardboard, and a child-size sloped shoe box

You will also need craft glue, tracing paper, colored corrugated craft cardboard, brass studs, transparent tape, and kraft paper.

1. Arrange and glue photographs onto piece of cardboard.
2. Carefully tear away top sheet from a piece of cardboard to expose ripples. Cutting pieces to overlap edges of photos ¼" and running ripples desired directions, cut pieces from cardboard to fit frame; arrange and glue in place.
3. Trace desired patterns, page 149, onto tracing paper; cut out. Using patterns, cut desired number of shapes from craft cardboard. Arrange and glue cutouts on frame; glue one stud to center of each cutout.
4. Cover box with kraft paper. Aligning bottom of box and frame, glue shoebox to back of frame for stand.

PRETTY CANDLE PLATTER

A china platter that's seen better days can be at your service again as a large candle dish. Glue flowers and greenery around the edge and dress up the candle with a pretty ribbon and charm.

DRIED FLOWER CANDLE DISH

Recycled item: china platter

You will also need a candle to fit platter, mood moss, dried flowers, hot glue gun, ribbon, embroidery floss to coordinate with ribbon, and a decorative gold charm.

1. Center candle on platter. Arrange moss and flowers around candle; glue to secure.
2. Tie ribbon into a bow around candle. Use floss to attach charm to knot of bow.

PILLOWCASE HANG-UP

CLOSET ORGANIZER

This "charm-ing" accent will organize your personal trinkets with feminine flair. A cinch to craft using a standard-size pillowcase and pretty handkerchiefs, the genteel accessory will also make a nice gift.

Recycled items: lace-edged embroidered pillowcase, heavy-duty coat hanger (we used a padded hanger), four 12" square handkerchiefs, buttons, and a scrap of ribbon

You will also need ⅛"w elastic, sewing thread to coordinate with handkerchiefs, and a hot glue gun.

1. Turn pillowcase wrong side out. Place pillowcase on a flat surface; center hanger along sewn end. Lightly draw along top edge of hanger on pillowcase extending lines to edges of pillowcase. Sewing through both layers and leaving an opening for hanger hook, sew along drawn lines. Trim corners from pillowcase along sewn lines. Turn pillowcase right side out.

2. For envelope-style pockets, press top of each handkerchief 2" to front; press bottom edge of handkerchief until even with top pressed edge (Fig. 1). Make two envelope-style pockets.

Fig. 1

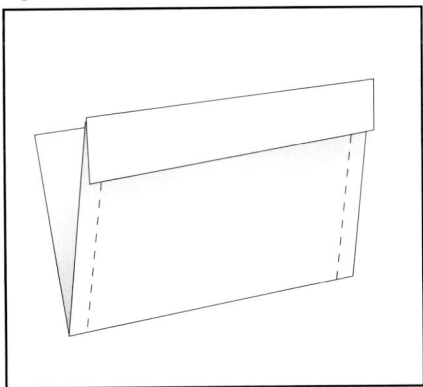

Fig. 2

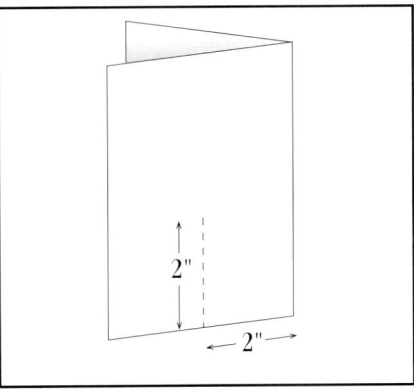

Fig. 3

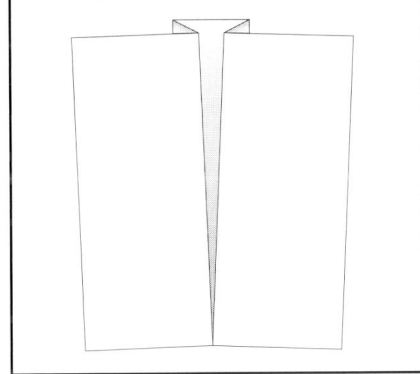

3. For pleated pockets, match right sides and press handkerchiefs in half from right to left. To sew pleat, sew a 2" long seam 2" from fold (Fig. 2). Press pleat flat (Fig. 3).

4. For elastic-topped pocket, cut a length of elastic the same size as bottom width of pocket. Stitching on wrong side of pocket 1" below top edge and gently stretching elastic to fit width of top edge of pocket, zigzag stitch elastic to pocket.

5. For buttoned-flap pocket, fold top edge of pocket 2" to right side. Sew button to center of flap to secure.

6. Arrange and pin pockets on pillowcase. Leaving flaps free, sew pockets along side and bottom edges to secure. Sew a button at each end of elastic.

7. Place organizer on hanger. Tie ribbon into a bow around hanger; glue button to knot of bow.

Bread Box Organizer

This ingenious organizer makes controlling paperwork easier than buttering toast! All you need is a little paint and pizzazz to convert an old metal bread box into an appealing floral space saver.

Bread Box Organizer

Recycled item: metal bread box

You will also need sandpaper; tack cloth; spray primer; green spray paint; stencil plastic; craft knife; cutting mat; removable tape; cream, light green, green, light purple, purple, and gold acrylic paint; 1/2" and 1" dia. foam daubers; assorted paintbrushes; and clear matte acrylic spray sealer.

Refer to Painting Techniques, page 157, before beginning project. Allow primer, paint, and sealer to dry after each application.

1. If necessary to remove rust, sand bread box and wipe with tack cloth. Apply primer, then two coats of green paint to inside and outside of box.
2. Follow *Stenciling*, page 157, and use pattern, page 149, to make stencil from plastic.
3. Use 1/2" dia. dauber to stencil petals purple, then use light purple paint to stencil highlights on petals; remove stencil.
4. Use 1" dia. dauber to paint a cream circle on each flower; use 1/2" dia. dauber to paint a light green dot at middle of each cream dot.
5. Paint a green *"C" Stroke* at center of each flower. Use end of a large paintbrush handle to paint a gold dot under each *"C" Stroke*; use end of a small paintbrush to paint a cream dot at center of each gold dot. Paint green tendrils. Add gold, purple, and cream dots in varying sizes to each flower, petals, and extending from flowers and tendrils.
6. Apply two to three coats of sealer to organizer.

SEASIDE TREASURE BOX

An old wooden frame and a shoebox are all you need to hold memories of a special day at the beach. Displaying shells and other treasures you collect on your outing, the container is lightly sanded to give it that breezy "just-washed-ashore" look.

SHADOWBOX FRAME

Recycled items: wooden picture frame (back removed) and a cardboard box to fit back of frame

You will also need black spray paint; white, light yellow, and yellow acrylic paint; paintbrushes; paste floor wax; sandpaper; tack cloth; handmade paper; spray adhesive; hot glue gun; assorted sea shells; and reindeer moss.

Allow paint to dry after each application.

1. Spray paint box black.
2. Paint frame yellow. Apply a thin layer of wax to frame, then paint frame light yellow. Lightly sand frame for a weathered look; wipe with tack cloth.
3. Make a wash using one part white paint to two parts water; apply wash to frame around opening.
4. Measure length and width of inside box bottom; cut a piece from paper the determined measurements. Apply spray adhesive to one side of paper; smooth onto inside bottom of box.
5. Arrange and glue shells and moss inside box.
6. Glue box to back of frame.

THE LATEST BUZZ

*D*on't bumble around trying to keep up with the busy bees in your family — post the latest buzz on this novelty message center. Crafted from a cabinet door, wire mesh, and clip-on bees, it'll take the sting out of your hectic schedule!

CABINET DOOR MESSAGE CENTER

Recycled items: cabinet door (our door measures 14"w x 27"h), chicken wire, and 1" dia. black buttons

You will also need wood filler; sandpaper; tack cloth; spray primer; white, yellow, and black acrylic paint; paintbrushes; stencil plastic; craft knife; cutting mat; wire cutters; yellow spray paint; clear acrylic spray sealer; upholstery tacks; hammer; hot glue gun; $1\frac{1}{2}$" and 2" long wooden egg halves; tracing paper; utility scissors; lightweight craft steel; and 1" long plastic clothespins.

Allow wood filler, primer, paint, and sealer to dry after each application.

1. Remove hardware from door. Fill holes with wood filler, sand when dry, then wipe with tack cloth. Apply primer to door.
2. Paint door black. Lightly mark an odd number of "stripes" along side trims of door; paint alternating stripes yellow. Paint white wavy lines over edges of stripes.
3. Using patterns, page 153, follow *Stenciling*, page 157, to stencil yellow words on top and bottom door trims. Use end of paintbrush handle to outline words with white dots. Apply two to three coats of sealer to door.
4. Measure height and width of center of door; add $\frac{1}{2}$" to each measurement. Use wire cutters to cut a piece from chicken wire the determined measurements. Spray paint chicken wire yellow.
5. Allowing excess wire to bow out from door; use tacks to secure chicken wire over center of door.
6. For each bumblebee, glue a button to back of egg half at wide end for head. Paint body with primer, then black paint. Paint yellow stripes on body. Paint a white wavy line or white dots along edges of stripes and along edges of head. Apply two to three coats of sealer to each bee.
7. Trace wing patterns, page 153, onto tracing paper; cut out. Draw around patterns two times (one in reverse) for each bee on craft steel; cut out. Cut two $\frac{1}{8}$" x 1" strips from steel for each set of antennae. Glue wings on bottom of body and antennae to head.
8. Glue large bees to door as desired. Glue clothespins to backs of small bees; clip bees to wire for note holders.

Timeworn Fruit Tray

Add timeworn color to wooden fruit with our simple painting technique. This classic arrangement will be a tantalizing table decoration.

Weathered Fruit

Recycled items: wooden tray, pieces of wooden fruit, and crocheted doily

You will also need desired colors of acrylic paint, paintbrushes, paste floor wax, and sandpaper.

Allow paint to dry after each application.

1. If necessary, wash tray and fruit; allow to dry. Paint tray and fruits desired colors.
2. Apply wax to tray and fruit; allow to dry. Lightly sand tray and fruit.
3. Place doily on tray. Arrange fruit on doily.

STACKED-UP CAKE STAND

Now you can have your cake and show it off in style, too! Keep an eye out at flea markets for old wooden dishes to stack and paint; add pizzazz with strands of faux pearls.

CAKE STAND

Recycled items: wooden bowl, wooden candleholder, and a wooden plate

You will also need wood glue, spray primer, desired colors of acrylic paint, paintbrushes, clear water-based polyurethane acrylic sealer, craft glue, and white string pearls.

Refer to Painting Techniques, page 157, before beginning project. Allow wood glue, primer, paint, and sealer to dry after each application.

1. Use wood glue to glue bowl, candleholder, and plate together to form cake stand.
2. Apply primer to stand. Paint stand as desired. Apply two to three coats of sealer to stand.
3. Trimming to fit, use craft glue to glue pearls around base of stand; allow to dry.

STRAW MAT MAKEOVERS

Weave a new look for old straw place mats by using them to transform assorted jars into candleholders and vases. You'll love the natural appeal of the simple wraps.

STRAW ENSEMBLE

Recycled items: three jars, straw place mats, straw, and buttons

You will also need craft glue, hot glue gun, and 1½"w ribbon.

Before cutting pieces from place mats, apply craft glue just inside cut line to hold straw in place; allow to dry. Use hot glue for all other gluing.

"BUTTONED" RIBBON VASE
1. Measure around jar and add ½"; measure height of jar. Use determined measurements to cut a piece from place mat; glue piece around jar.
2. Overlapping ends and trimming to fit, glue ribbon around vase; glue buttons to ribbon.

VASE WITH BOW
1. Measure around jar and add ½"; measure height of jar. Use determined measurements to cut a piece from place mat; glue piece around jar.
2. Tie a length of ribbon into a bow around top of jar; glue a button to knot of bow.

CANDLEHOLDER
1. Measure height of jar; add ½". Cut pieces of straw the determined measurement. With stems extending above top of jar, glue stems around jar.
2. Measure around jar; add ½". Cut two ¾"w strips from place mat by the determined measurement. Overlapping ends, glue strips around top and bottom of candleholder.
3. Glue buttons to candleholder.

NOSTALGIC MAGAZINE RACK

An old tin ceiling tile provides a handy keeping place for casual reading materials. A rusty star and a string of timeworn buttons add to the nostalgic look of this hanging accessory.

MAGAZINE RACK

Recycled items: 12" x 25" tin ceiling tile and assorted buttons

You will also need clear acrylic spray sealer, hammer, awl, black medium-gauge craft wire, wire cutters, and one 5" tall rusted tin star cutout.

1. Apply two to three coats of sealer to tile; allow to dry.
2. Referring to Fig. 1, mark center of tile on wrong side. Use hammer and awl to punch holes along edges of tile.

Fig. 1

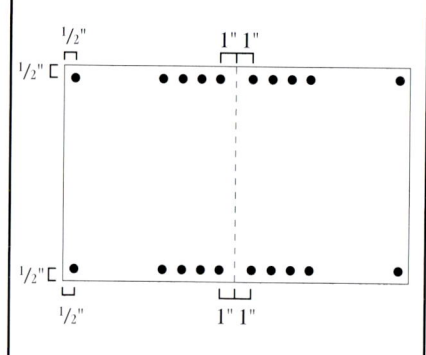

3. To form rack, gently bend tile along mark.
4. Lace a length of wire through holes on each side of rack; twist wire around itself to secure. Trim wire ends.
5. Measure width of rack; add 4". Cut a length of wire the determined measurement; thread buttons onto wire. Thread ends of wire through holes in front corners of rack. Twist wire around itself to secure; trim ends. Use hammer and awl to punch a hole in one point of star. Use wire to attach star to center of button swag.

SPICY JEWELRY RACK

*S*easoned collectors will appreciate this clever jewelry keeper that's fashioned from a spice rack, drawer pulls, and dollhouse trim. Add a pinch of glue and a dash of paint for a display case that's ideal for necklaces, rings, and bracelets.

SPICE RACK JEWELRY ORGANIZER

Recycled item: wooden 2-shelf spice rack

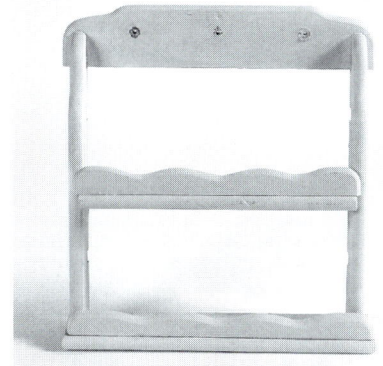

You will also need a saw; wooden dollhouse trim; wood glue; drill and bits; three drawer pulls; spray primer; white, yellow, and green acrylic paint; paintbrushes; and clear acrylic spray sealer.

Refer to Painting Techniques, page 157, before beginning project. Allow wood glue, primer, paint, and sealer to dry after each application.

1. For organizer, turn rack upside down. Measure width of spice rack; cut two pieces of trim the determined measurement. Glue trim pieces across back of rack between shelves.

2. Drill three holes along bottom of organizer; attach drawer pulls to organizer.

3. Apply primer, then white paint to organizer. *Dry Brush* yellow on organizer as desired.

4. Apply two to three coats of sealer to organizer.

85

"Tea-Lightful" Lamp

*W*ith *its tarnished finish, this transformed teapot lamp will light the way down memory lane. A few hardware-store essentials are all you need to finish it.*

TEAPOT LAMP

Recycled item: metal teapot

You will also need a hacksaw, welding compound, drill with 3/8" dia. high-speed drill bit; 1/8" IP lamp parts from electrical supply store: two 2" lengths of threaded pipe, four lock nuts, harp cradle, socket base with shell, electrical cord with male plug on one end, lamp harp; and a lampshade.

If your teapot does not have a knob, purchase a finial to fit lamp harp. Refer to Diagram to assemble lamp.

1. Remove lid from teapot. Use hacksaw to remove knob from teapot lid. Use welding compound to attach one lock nut to bottom of knob for lamp finial.
2. Drill hole through center top of lid and center bottom of pot; replace lid.
3. Place one 2" long threaded pipe piece through hole at bottom of pot. Twist one lock nut onto pipe at bottom outside of pot until lock nut is flush with end of pipe; twist one lock nut onto pipe inside pot until tight against bottom of pot.
4. Place remaining pipe through hole in lid. Twist one lock nut 1" onto pipe inside lid; twist remaining lock nut onto pipe until tight against top of lid.
5. Twist harp cradle, then socket base, onto top of pipe until tight against lock nut. Loosen screws on socket shell. Thread electrical cord through pipe from bottom to lid. Wrap one wire on cord around one screw on socket shell twice; tighten screw. Repeat to attach remaining wire to opposite side. Snap socket shell into socket base.
6. Place harp, shade, and finial on lamp.

DIAGRAM

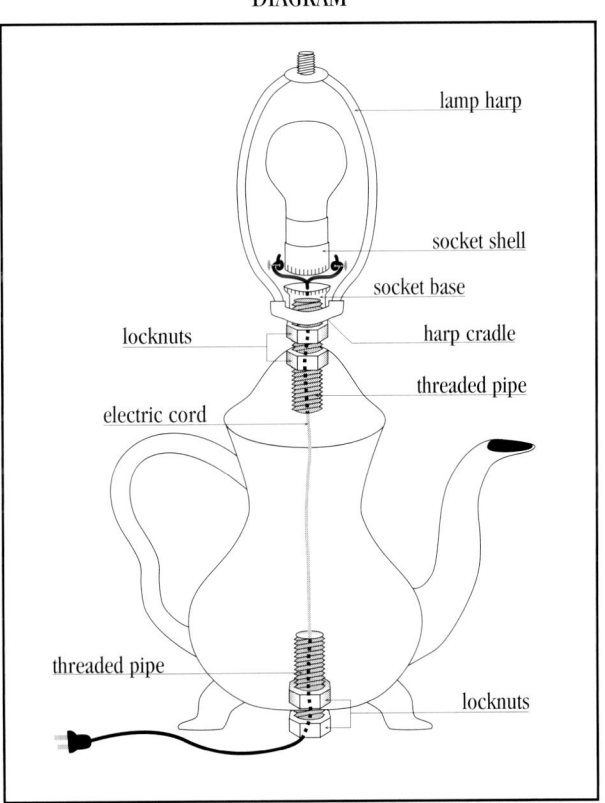

PAGE-TURNING PRINTS

*Y*ou'll turn a new page in children's décor when you decoupage and frame a touching scene and classic quotation from a well-loved storybook. Embellish the timeless illustrations with buttons and ribbons for extra charm.

CHILDREN'S BOOK FRAMED PRINT

Recycled items: wooden picture frame, a child's illustrated book, and a button.

You will also need primer, desired color of acrylic paint, paintbrush, mat board, decoupage glue, wood-tone spray, spray mount adhesive, hot glue gun, and wire-edged ribbon.

Allow primer, paint, decoupage glue, and wood-tone spray to dry after each application.

1. Apply primer to frame; paint frame desired color.
2. Cut a piece of mat board to fit in frame.
3. Cut desired illustration and verse from book, trimming verse to fit on frame and illustration to fit on mat board.
4. Follow *Decoupage*, page 157, to adhere verse on frame. Apply a light coat of wood-tone spray to frame and verse.
5. Apply spray mount to wrong side of illustration; center and smooth onto mat board.
6. Hot glue mat board in frame opening.
7. Tie ribbon into a bow; hot glue to frame. Hot glue button to knot of bow.

"CAN-DID" FRAME

Preserve a favorite image of beauty for years to come in this clever floral frame! Create the decorative flowers out of soda cans and metal bottle caps from your recycling bin.

BEVERAGE CAN FRAME

Recycled items: five 12-oz. aluminum beverage cans, four metal bottle caps, and a wide wooden picture frame

You will also need utility scissors, hammer, tracing paper, transfer paper, craft foam, stylus, spray primer, brown spray paint, mat board and cardboard (for backing) to fit in frame, paste floor wax, green acrylic paint, paintbrushes, fine-grit sandpaper, tack cloth, hot glue gun, hammer, 1/2" long brass nails, clear acrylic spray sealer, clear tape, and a photograph to fit in mat board opening.

Refer to Transferring a Pattern, page 157, before beginning project. Allow primer, paint, and sealer to dry after each application.

1. Cut through openings in beverage cans and down to bottom rims; cut away and discard tops and bottoms of cans. Flatten can pieces. Use hammer to flatten bottle caps for flower centers.
2. Trace patterns, page 154, onto tracing paper; cut out. Use patterns to cut out four flowers and eight leaves from can pieces (cut four leaves in reverse).
3. To emboss each flower and leaf, use transfer paper to transfer detail lines from patterns to printed sides of flowers and leaves. Place shapes, printed side up, on craft foam. Pressing firmly to make indentions, use stylus to trace over detail lines.
4. Arrange and glue flowers and leaves on frame. Nail leaves to secure; nail one flower center to each flower.
5. Apply primer, then brown spray paint to frame and mat. Randomly apply wax to frame and mat pieces, then paint green. Lightly sand pieces for a weathered look and wipe with tack cloth. Apply two to three coats of sealer to frame.
6. Tape photograph in opening in mat; glue mat, then cardboard backing to back of frame.

Show the softer side of your accessories with unique creations guaranteed to spread handmade warmth throughout the home. Old clothing, vintage fabrics, and linens become impressive new sachets, pillows, quilts, wall hangings, and more! With these great ideas for easy-to-make decorating accents and gifts, you'll never discard another scrap of cloth again!

SHIRT-PATCH WRAP

Warm up this winter by putting on another layer of clothes! Accented with buttons and bow-tie appliqués, a patchwork of old shirts becomes an eye-catching cover-up.

SHIRT PATCHWORK QUILT

Recycled items: shirts and buttons

You will also need fabric for borders and backing, paper-backed fusible web, and batting.

Use a $1/4$" seam allowance for all sewing unless otherwise indicated.

1. For quilt top, cut thirty-nine $4^{1}/_{2}$" x 9" rectangles from shirts. Matching right sides and long edges, sew thirteen rectangles together to make a row; repeat to make three rows.
2. From border fabric, cut two $3^{1}/_{2}$" x 53" sashing strips and two $5^{1}/_{2}$" x 53" side border strips. Matching right sides and long edges, sew sashing strips between rows; sew border strips to outer edges.
3. Cut two $5^{1}/_{2}$" x 42" strips for top and bottom borders. Matching right sides and long edges, sew borders in place.
4. Referring to *Fusible Appliqués*, page 156, use bow tie pattern, page 146, to make sixteen appliqués from remaining shirt pieces. Evenly spacing three bow ties on each short border and five bow ties on each long border, fuse appliqués in place; follow *Machine Appliqué*, page 156, to stitch appliqués in place.
5. Cut batting and backing fabric 2" larger on each side than quilt top. To assemble quilt, place backing wrong side up on a flat surface. Layer batting, then quilt top right side up on backing. Baste along edges to secure.
6. To make pieced binding, cut remaining shirt scraps into pieces $2^{1}/_{2}$"w and 3" to 9" in length. Sew $2^{1}/_{2}$"w edges to make two 45" top and two 56" side binding pieces. Matching long edges and wrong sides, press binding pieces in half.
7. Matching raw edges, sew top and bottom binding pieces to right side of quilt. If necessary, trim ends of binding even with edges of quilt. Fold binding over to quilt backing and pin pressed edges in place, covering stitching line; hand sew binding to backing. Remove pins.
8. Leaving $1^{1}/_{2}$" at each end, stitch side binding pieces to right side of quilt. Trim ends of binding $1/2$" longer than bound edges. Fold each short end of binding $1/2$" to wrong side. Fold binding over to backing and stitch in place; remove pins.
9. Stitch buttons to quilt as desired.

SIMPLE SACHETS

94

Let the sweet aroma of these handmade sachets remind a special lady that you appreciate her. Fashioned from embroidered handkerchiefs and crocheted doilies from the flea-market, the simple potpourri holders will make ideal gifts for Valentine's Day or Mother's Day.

SACHETS

BOW SACHET

Recycled item: embroidered linen (we used a 7" x 11" handkerchief) and a button

You will also need dried potpourri, hot glue gun, 3" of $1^{1}/_{4}$"w wire-edged ribbon, 3" of $^{1}/_{2}$"w satin ribbon, and 5" of $^{1}/_{8}$"w satin ribbon.

1. Matching short edges and wrong sides, fold linen in half. Leaving an opening for filling, sew edges together.
2. Lightly fill sachet with potpourri; sew opening closed.
3. Overlapping and gluing ends at back, wrap $1^{1}/_{4}$"w ribbon, then $^{1}/_{2}$"w ribbon around center of sachet. Tie $^{1}/_{8}$"w ribbon into a bow. Glue bow, then button to ribbon.

ENVELOPE SACHET

Recycled item: 8" square handkerchief and a button

You will also need dried potpourri and 5" of $^{1}/_{8}$"w satin ribbon.

1. Place handkerchief right side down on a flat surface. Refer to Fig. 1 to overlap two opposite corners about 2" at center of handkerchief.

Fig. 1

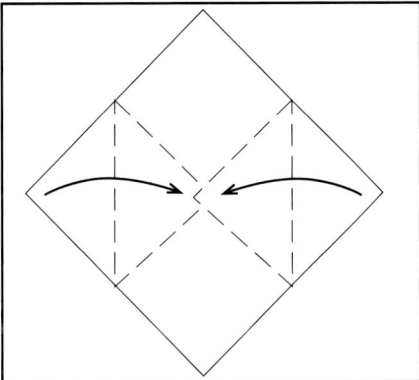

2. Fold bottom point of handkerchief up to overlapped points, then fold bottom edge to bottom corners of flaps (Fig. 2).

Fig. 2

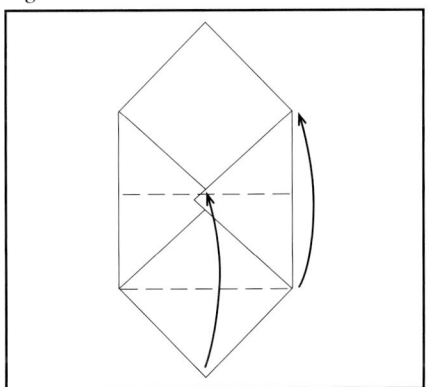

3. Lightly fill envelope with potpourri. Fold top corner down over overlapped area; sew button to corner through all layers to secure.

4. Tie ribbon into a bow; sew behind button.

ROSE-TOPPED SACHET

Recycled items: 10" dia. round lacy doily and a $2^{1}/_{2}$"h votive holder

You will also need $^{1}/_{8}$"w satin ribbon, dried potpourri, 10" of $^{5}/_{8}$"w satin ribbon, hot glue gun, $1^{1}/_{2}$"w wire-edged ribbon, and two artificial leaves.

1. Leaving 3" at beginning and end of ribbon free, thread $^{1}/_{8}$"w ribbon through outer holes along edges of doily.
2. Place votive holder at center of doily; fill with potpourri. Pull ribbon ends to gather doily over votive holder; tie ribbon into a bow to secure gathers.
3. Tie $^{5}/_{8}$"w ribbon into a bow; glue over gathers of doily.
4. For rose, gather one edge of wired ribbon until gathered edge measures 10" long. Spot glue at ends of ribbon to secure; trim wire ends. Fold one corner of ribbon to meet gathered edge (Fig. 3). Wrap ribbon around itself to form a rose; glue end to secure.

Fig. 3

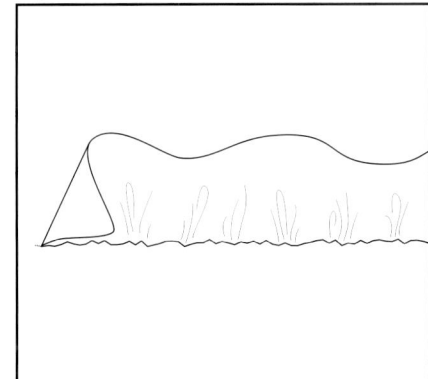

5. Glue rose, then leaves to knot of bow.

GOOD-NIGHT SACHETS

If you hate to throw away your old nighties, you'll love rescuing them to make these satiny sachet bags! You can use the spaghetti straps as coordinating ties.

NIGHTIE SACHET BAGS

Recycled items: two coordinating nightgowns with spaghetti straps

Use a ½" seam allowance for all sewing unless otherwise indicated.

1. From nightgowns, cut a 6" x 11" rectangle and a 2" x 11" strip for band. Press one long edge of band ½" to wrong side. Matching long, raw edges, pin right side of band to wrong side of rectangle; sew pieces together along long edge. Fold band to right side at seam; top stitch along pressed edge to secure.

2. For ties, cut one strap from nightgown. Fold strap in half. Pin fold to right side of bag 1½" from top edge (Fig. 1).

Fig. 1

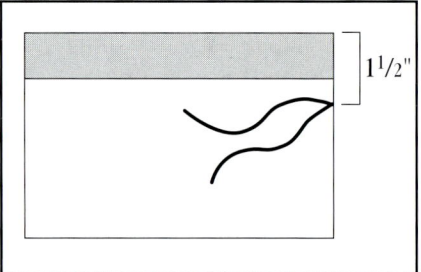

3. Matching short edges and right sides, fold bag in half; sew side and bottom of bag together. Turn bag right side out; press.

"WELL-SUITED" FRAME

Now Dad can enjoy his favorite suits even after he wears them out! Simply arrange collars, cuffs, and sleeves in a frame and add some men's accessories. You'll create a stylish wall hanging the whole family will appreciate.

MEN'S SUIT COLLAGE

Recycled items: large wooden picture frame, heavy-weight corrugated cardboard, men's wool suits, and items to decorate collage

You will also need muslin, paper-backed fusible web, clear nylon thread, spray adhesive, and a staple gun.

1. Cut pieces of muslin and cardboard to fit frame opening.
2. Cut lapels, pockets, sleeves, and cuffs from suits. Follow manufacturer's instructions to fuse web to wrong side of pieces.
3. Overlapping as desired, arrange and fuse suit pieces on muslin. Use clear thread and a zigzag stitch to sew pieces along raw edges. 
4. Apply spray adhesive to back of muslin; smooth onto cardboard piece. Use staple gun to attach covered cardboard to back of frame.
5. Use clear thread to attach additional decorative items to collage.

GRACEFUL CHAIR COVERS

Add a touch of whimsy to a plain chair with graceful covers made using a ruffled bedsheet. These toppers are so appealing, guests will take a seat without your asking!

CHAIR COVERS

Recycled items: lace-trimmed table runner slightly narrower than chairback and a print bedsheet with a ruffled edge

You will also need paper-backed fusible web and 1" thick foam.

Use a $1/2$" seam allowance for all sewing unless otherwise indicated.

1. For chair cushion pattern, draw around seat on paper. Mark front of seat on pattern. Use pattern to cut shape from foam. Using pattern, cut seat bottom from straight end of sheet 1" larger than pattern. Press front edge $1/2$" to wrong side; stitch in place. Aligning front edge of pattern with ruffle seam on sheet, refer to Fig. 1 to cut out seat top 1" larger than pattern.

Fig. 1

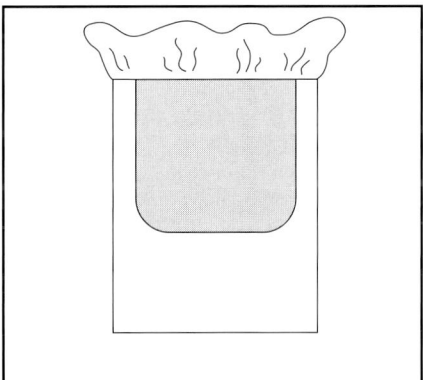

2. Matching right sides and raw edges, sew seat cover pieces together along raw edges. Clip seam allowance and turn right side out; press. Insert foam in cover and place on chair.

3. For chairback cover, measure height of chairback; add 1". Measure width of chairback; add 2". With ruffled edge of sheet at bottom of cover, cut two pieces from sheet the determined measurements (Fig. 2).

Fig. 2

4. Determine desired length for chairback overlay and add $1/2$"; cut length from one end of table runner. Fuse web to wrong side of remaining sheet under desired motif. Cut out motif, then fuse to right side of overlay.

5. Matching raw edges, layer overlay between right sides of chairback cover pieces. Being careful not to catch sides of overlay in seam, sew pieces together along top and side edges; turn right side out, press, and place on chair.

Prom-Dress Pillows

Prom night will live on in more than photo albums when these pillows become a part of the daily décor. These easy-to-sew accents will preserve precious memories while inviting many conversational opportunities to relive that unforgettable gala.

PROM-DRESS PILLOWS

Recycled items: formal dresses

You will also need fabric for pillow front and back, matching sewing thread, $3/8$" dia. cording, straight pins, and polyester fiberfill.

Match right sides and use a $1/2$" seam allowance for all sewing unless otherwise indicated.

WELTED PILLOW

1. Cut two 14" squares from fabric for pillow front and pillow back. Cut a 14" square from desired area of dress for pillow front overlay. Baste overlay to right side of pillow front.

2. For welting, cut a 57" piece of cording. Piecing as necessary, cut a $2^1/2$"w by $4^1/2$ yd. strip from dress. Press one end $1/2$" to wrong side. Matching wrong sides and long edges and beginning $1/2$" from pressed end, baste long edges together to make tube.

3. Thread cording through tube, gathering tube to fit length of cording. Beginning with unpressed end and matching raw edges, pin welting to right side of pillow front (Fig. 1).

Fig. 1

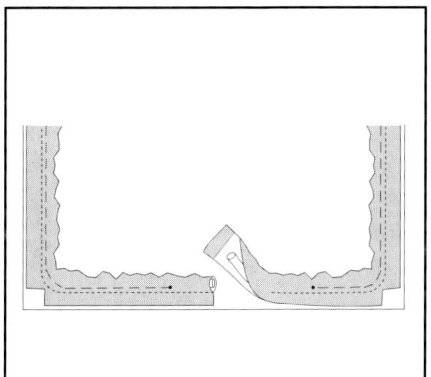

4. Trimming to fit and adjusting gathers as necessary, insert unfinished end of welting into folded end of welting (Fig. 2). Baste welting in place; remove pins.

Fig. 2

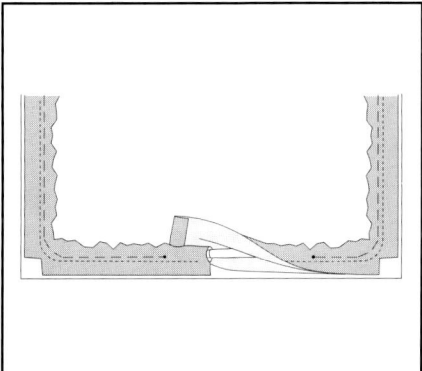

5. Leaving an opening for turning, sew pillow pieces together. Clip corners and turn right side out. Stuff pillow with fiberfill and sew opening closed.

RUFFLED PILLOW

1. Cut two $12^1/2$" x $17^1/2$" pieces from fabric for pillow front and pillow back. Cut one $12^1/2$" x $17^1/2$" piece from desired area of dress for pillow front overlay. Baste overlay to right side of pillow front.

2. Piecing as necessary, cut a 7"w by $4^1/2$ yd. strip from dress. Matching right sides, sew short edges of ruffle together to form a large circle; press seam allowance open. Matching wrong sides and raw edges, press ruffle piece in half lengthwise. To gather ruffle, baste $1/4$" and $3/8$" from raw edges; pull thread, drawing up gathers to fit pillow front. Matching raw edges, baste ruffle to right side of pillow front.

3. Leaving an opening for turning, sew pillow pieces together. Clip corners and turn right side out. Stuff pillow with fiberfill and sew opening closed.

HANKIE TABLE TOPPER

Satisfy your "hankering" for vintage décor with an heirloom-quality table topper. Several delicate handkerchiefs are sewn together to form the frilly table drape. Assorted buttons complete the quaint look in a snap!

HANKIE TABLE TOPPER

Recycled items: assorted handkerchiefs and buttons

You will also need clear nylon sewing thread.

1. Overlapping edges ¼", arrange handkerchiefs to desired size of topper; pin in place. Use nylon thread and a ¼"w zigzag stitch to sew handkerchiefs together.
2. Sew buttons to corners of handkerchiefs as desired.

PLACE MATS UNDERFOOT!

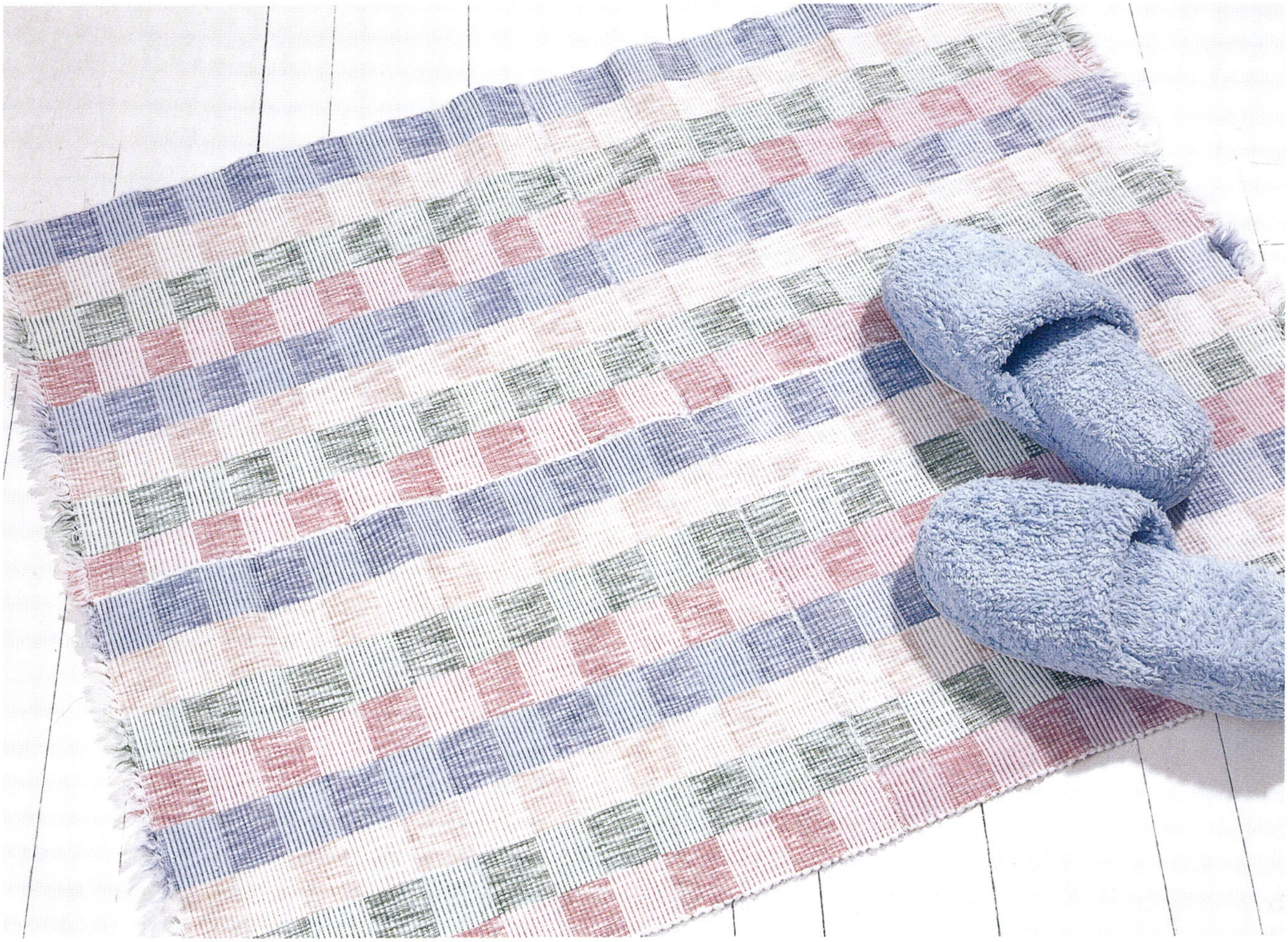

This throw rug is "sew" simple to create, you won't miss a step! Four woven place mats are stitched together to make the quick-and-easy floor covering.

PLACE MAT THROW RUG

Recycled items: four woven place mats with fringed ends

You will also need coordinating heavy-duty thread.

1. For each half section, match unfringed edges of two place mats together, right side up; use a zigzag stitch to sew together. Repeat for remaining two place mats.

2. Carefully trim fringe from one edge of each section. Matching trimmed edges, place sections together, right sides up; use a zigzag stitch to sew together.

COUNTRY GARDEN CUSHION

Our homespun pillow will turn your thinking about socks inside out! We used coffee-dyed white socks and simple embroidery stitches to make the checkerboard pattern on this quaint, garden-appliqué pillow.

SOCK APPLIQUÉ PILLOW

Recycled items: five adult-size white socks

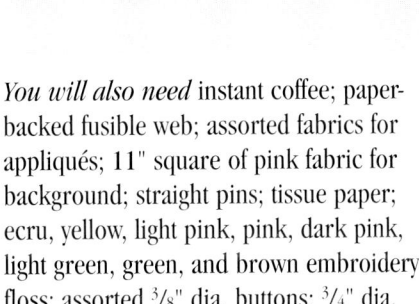

You will also need instant coffee; paper-backed fusible web; assorted fabrics for appliqués; 11" square of pink fabric for background; straight pins; tissue paper; ecru, yellow, light pink, pink, dark pink, light green, green, and brown embroidery floss; assorted ³⁄₈" dia. buttons; ³⁄₄" dia. button; two 13" squares of cotton batting; and an 8" square pillow form.

Before beginning project, refer to Embroidery Stitches, page 159, and use two strands of floss for all embroidery unless otherwise indicated.

1. Follow *Coffee Dyeing*, page 156, to dye socks. Cut five 3" squares from socks.
2. Using patterns, page 148, follow *Fusible Appliqués*, page 156, to make four heart appliqués from socks and one each flowerpot, wheelbarrow, basket, and planter appliqué from assorted fabrics.
3. For pillow top, leaving a 1" wide fabric border, arrange and pin squares, then arrange and fuse heart appliqués on background fabric. Work *Blanket Stitches* along edges of squares. Work *Running Stitches* along edges of hearts and across background "squares" to connect sock squares.
4. Fuse remaining appliqués on pillow top.
5. Trace embroidery patterns, page 148, onto tissue paper. Arrange and pin patterns on pillow top. Refer to stitch key, page 148, to embroider designs. Carefully remove paper.
6. Use brown floss to sew one ³⁄₈" dia. button to each corner of square appliqués and ³⁄₄" dia. button to wheelbarrow for tire. Center and pin pillow top on one batting square; pin in place.
7. Matching wrong sides, pin batting pieces together. Leaving an opening for stuffing, use ecru floss to work *Running Stitches* through all layers ¹⁄₄" from edge of background square; insert pillow form. Continue *Running Stitches* to sew opening closed.

BABY'S KEEPSAKE QUILT

Little ones grow up quickly, so craft a memory quilt to capture those special moments. Use our simple piecing techniques to create the precious wall hanging, then give it life by embellishing with Baby's keepsakes.

BABY'S WALL QUILT

Recycled items: baby clothing, buttons, trims, baby blanket, fabrics, and assorted baby items

You will also need photo transfer paper, embroidery floss, jumbo rickrack, fabric for backing, batting, and ribbon.

CUTTING OUT THE PIECES
When cutting pieces for quilt from clothing, position cuts to incorporate design elements such as embroidery or appliqués. Use a 1/4" seam allowance for all sewing unless otherwise indicated.

From fabrics and clothing, cut a 10½" x 12½" rectangle for Section A, nine light and nine dark 2½" squares for Section B, an 8½" square for Section C, eight light and eight dark 2⅞" squares for Sections D and I, a 4½" x 12½" rectangle for Section E, an 8½" x 9½" rectangle for Section F, a 3½" x 8½" rectangle for Section G, a 12½" square for Section H, an 8½" square for Section J, and two 4½" x 12½" rectangles for Sections K and L.

MAKING THE PIECED SECTIONS
Use a ¼" seam allowance for all piecing. Press seam allowances to one side toward darker fabric.

1. Alternating light and dark squares, sew six 2½" squares for Section B together to form a strip; make three strips. Alternating direction of center strip, sew strips together to make Section B.
2. Place one light and one dark 2⅞" square for Section D right sides together. Referring to Fig. 1, draw a diagonal line on wrong side of lighter square; stitch ¼" from each side of line. Cut along drawn line; open and press each triangle-square. Repeat with remaining 2⅞" squares to make a total of 16 triangle-squares. Sew four triangle-squares together to make pinwheel block; make four pinwheel blocks. Sew each pair of pinwheel blocks together to make Sections D and I.

Fig. 1

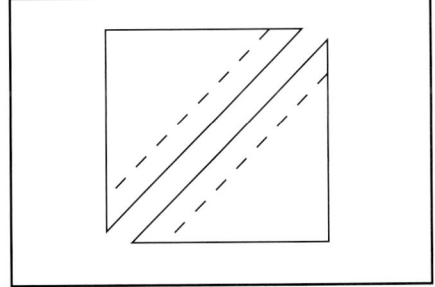

EMBELLISHING THE SECTIONS
Refer to Embroidery Stitches, page 159, before embellishing the sections. Adapt the instructions to work with your own memorabilia.

1. For Section A, make three yo-yo flowers. For each flower, cut a 3½" dia. circle from fabric. Turn raw edge of circle ¼" to wrong side. Using a double strand of thread, work *Running Stitches* along folded edge. Pull thread to tightly gather circle; knot thread and trim ends. Flatten circle. Repeat using 2" dia. circles to make three flower centers. Matching gathered sides, *Blind Stitch* flower center to flowers. Using patterns, page 147, follow *Hand Appliqué*, page 157, to appliqué stems, leaves, and yo-yo flowers in place. Write name with pencil. Using three strands of floss, work *Stem Stitches* over name.
2. Following manufacturer's instructions, use photo transfer paper to transfer images from birth announcement and baby book to Sections C, F, and K, adding embroidered dates or other details as desired.
3. Use *Blind Stitches* to stitch clothing items in place, on Sections E, H, and J.

ASSEMBLING THE QUILT TOP
Refer to Diagram to assemble quilt top.

1. Sew Sections C and D together; add Section B, then A to make Row 1.
2. Sew Sections F and G together; add Section E, then H to make Row 2.
3. Sew Sections K and L together; add Section J, then I to make Row 3.
4. Sew rows together to complete quilt top.

DIAGRAM

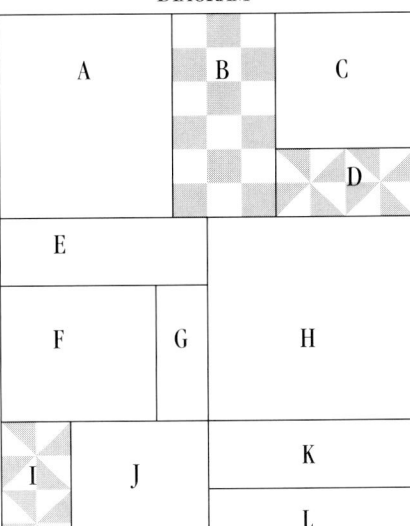

FINISHING THE QUILT

1. Baste rickrack ¼" from raw edge on right side of quilt top.
2. For hanging sleeve, cut a 6½" x 23" strip from backing fabric. Press ends ¼" to wrong side two times; top stitch to secure. Matching wrong sides and long edges, press strip in half. Center raw edges of hanging sleeve along top edge on right side of backing; baste in place.
3. Cut backing fabric and batting same size as quilt top. Baste batting to wrong side of backing. Matching right sides and leaving an opening for turning, sew backing and top together. Trim corners and turn right side out; sew opening closed. *Blind Stitch*, page 159, pressed edge of hanging sleeve to back of quilt.
4. Sew buttons and ribbon tied items as desired on quilt.

Comfy Chenille Cushion

Wrap up this comfy cushion in no time! The cozy throw pillow is easily created from a chenille bedspread and an embroidered linen bread cloth. Buttons and a bow provide the perfect finishing touches to tie this project together.

Chenille Pillow

Recycled items: chenille bedspread and one 20" cross-shaped bread cloth

You will also need polyester fiberfill; two 24" lengths of $1/4$"w sheer ribbon; one each $5/8$", $3/4$", and $1 1/8$" dia. flat buttons; long needle; and heavy-duty thread.

1. For pillow, cut two 11" squares from bedspread. Matching right sides, leaving an opening for turning, and using a $1/2$" seam allowance, sew pieces together. Refer to Fig. 1 to sew across each corner of pillow; trim corners and turn pillow right side out.

Fig. 1

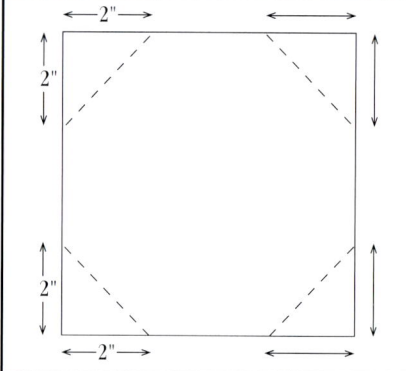

2. Stuff pillow with fiberfill, then sew opening closed.
3. Place bread cloth wrong side up on a flat surface. Center pillow on bread cloth. Wrap ends of bread cloth to center of pillow; tack ends in place.

4. Thread ribbons through holes in $3/4$" dia. button; leave ends loose. Referring to Fig. 2, sew through buttons at center of pillow. Pull threads tight to cinch, then knot thread ends to secure. Tie ribbons into a bow.

Fig. 2

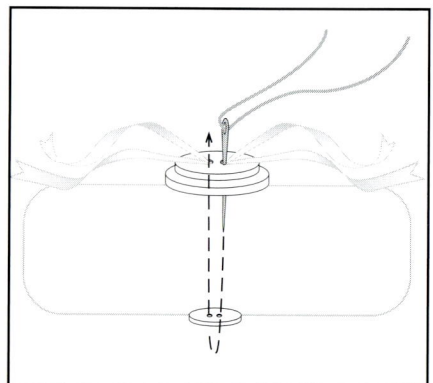

SCALLOPED SHELF EDGING

Refresh the look of your bathroom by lining shelves with a vinyl tablecloth embellished with scallops of castoff buttons. Practical and pretty, the water-resistant edging will help protect the shelves from water spots.

SHELF EDGING

Recycled items: vinyl tablecloth and buttons

You will also need tracing paper and a hot glue gun.

1. For each liner, cut a piece from tablecloth to fit shelf plus a 4" drop.
2. Trace edging pattern, page 151, onto tracing paper; cut out. Use pattern to cut scallops along edges of drop.
3. Glue buttons to right side of liner along edges of scallops.

PATCHWORK PILLOWS

Pay homage to your favorite quilter by piecing these patchwork pillows to support her back as she sews. Novice stitchers will easily gain experience with these projects, which are ingeniously made out of motifs from canvas carry-alls and assorted fabrics.

CANVAS BAG PILLOWS

Recycled items: canvas bags with motifs

For each pillow, you will also need assorted fabrics to coordinate with motif on bag and polyester fiberfill.

Match right sides of fabrics and use a ¼" seam allowance for all sewing. When sewing strips to center pieces, align one long edge of each strip with one edge of center piece. After stitching, trim ends of strips even with center piece.

1. For each pillow front, cut desired area from bag; include a ¼" seam allowance on each side of piece.

2. For pillow with pieced border, cut 2½"w fabric strips in lengths varying from 2" to 3½". Sew 2½" edges of pieces together to form a strip. Refer to Fig. 1 to sew strip to sides, then to top and bottom of center piece. Cut 2½"w fabric strips; sew to sides, then top and bottom of center piece to complete pillow front.

Fig. 1

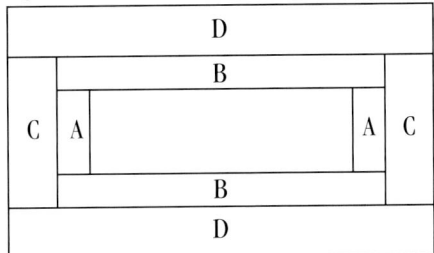

3. For courthouse steps pillow, cut 1½"w and 2½"w fabric strips. Referring to Fig. 2, sew 1½"w strips to sides, then top and bottom of center piece. Repeat using 2½"w strips to complete pillow front.

Fig. 2

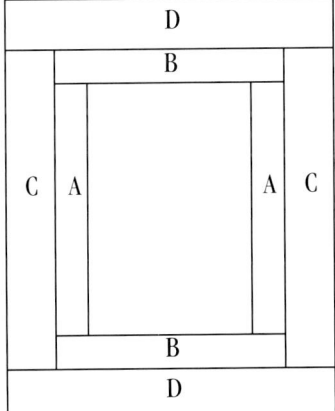

4. For log cabin pillow, cut 2½"w fabric strips. Referring to Fig. 3, begin on one side and work around center piece to sew strips to center until there are three strips on each side to complete pillow front.

Fig. 3

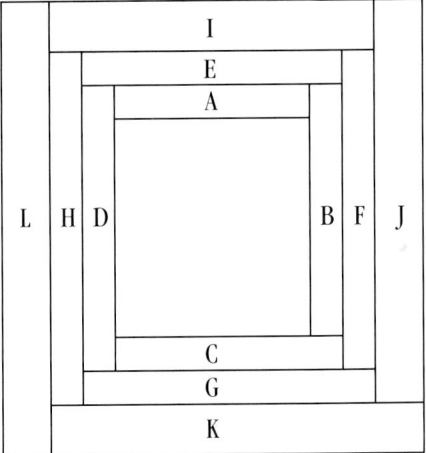

5. To complete each pillow, cut a pillow back the same size as pieced pillow front. Leaving an opening for turning, sew pillow front and back together; clip corners and turn right side out. Stuff pillow with fiberfill and sew opening closed.

Vintage Doily Pillow

A vintage doily takes center stage on this bolstered beauty. Adorned with scraps of coordinating fabric and a flourish of tassels, the classic pillow offers both comfort and charm.

VINTAGE DOILY PILLOW

Recycled items: fabrics, doily, and two large buttons

You will also need embroidery floss, paper-backed fusible web, pinking shears, $1/8$" and $5/8$" dia. cord, needle with large eye and blunt point, two 25mm wooden beads with large holes, craft glue, two tassels, and polyester fiberfill.

1. From fabrics, cut a piece $1/2$" larger on all sides than doily for background, one 15" x 24" center band, two $6^{1}/_{2}$" x 24" strips for pillow ends, and two $3^{1}/_{2}$" x 24" strips for welting.
2. Fuse web to wrong side of background; remove paper backing. Center doily on background. Using three strands of floss, work *Running Stitches*, page 154, $1/8$" inside edge of doily. Use pinking shears to cut out background fabric $1/4$" outside edge of doily. Center layered doily on band and fuse in place.
3. Cut two 24" lengths of $5/8$" dia. cord. Center each cord lengthwise on wrong side of one fabric strip for welting; fold fabric over cord. Use a zipper foot to sew close to cord; trim seam allowance to $1/2$". Matching right sides and long edges and enclosing welting, use a $1/2$" seam allowance to sew center band and pillow end pieces together; press.
4. Matching right sides and short edges, fold pillow cover in half; sew along long edges to form a tube. Turn tube right side out.
5. For casing, press ends of tube $1/4$" to wrong side; press again $3/4$" to wrong side. Leaving an opening to thread cord through, sew in place along pressed edge.
6. For each tassel, cut tassel hanger in half at center. Thread hanger through hole in bead and holes in one button; knot to secure.
7. Tear a $1/2$" wide strip from fabric; thread needle with strip. Working fabric through hole, wrap each bead with fabric, glue end in hole to secure.
8. Cut two 18" lengths of $1/8$" dia. cord. Using needle, thread cord through casing at each end of pillow. Placing button of one tassel in pillow, pull cord to gather end tightly between button and bead; knot cord and trim ends. Stuff pillow with fiberfill, then repeat to gather remaining end of pillow.

DRAPERY TABLE MATS

Be pleasantly reminded of warm, breezy afternoons each time you sip tea over these dainty drapery-panel place mats. Coordinating lace doilies provide decorative detail while a cleverly constructed napkin ring adds the finishing touch.

DRAPERY PLACE MATS

Recycled items: drapery panel, laces, decorative trims, doilies to coordinate with drapery panel, and handkerchiefs

You will also need low-loft polyester batting, satin cord with flange, and coordinating heavy-duty sewing thread.

1. For each place mat, cut one piece from batting and two pieces from drapery panel 13" x 19".
2. Cutting and trimming as necessary, sew laces, trims, and doilies to right side of one drapery piece as desired. For napkin ring, press one end of a 5" length of lace $1/2$" to wrong side. Matching unpressed end with edge of place mat, pin, then sew napkin ring 6" from bottom edge of place mat; tack pressed end to mat.
3. Matching raw edge of flange on cord with raw edges of embellished drapery panel piece, pin cord around mat piece; baste in place. Matching right sides, layer drapery pieces together. Layer batting on top of drapery pieces. Leaving an opening for turning, use a zipper foot to sew pieces together; turn right side out and sew opening closed.
4. Fold a handkerchief and place in napkin ring for napkin.

SHIRT-POCKET ORGANIZER

Pocket dozens of compliments while organizing a cluttered spot with this handsome wall hanging. "Tailored" from the pockets and button cuffs of long-sleeve shirts on a fabric backing of your choosing, this organizer is a perfect fit for an office based at work or at home.

SHIRT-POCKET WALL HANGING

Recycled items: nine long-sleeved shirts with pockets and button cuffs

You will also need utility scissors, translucent stencil plastic, two 28" squares of fabric for background and backing (may be cut from shirt backs, piecing as necessary), hot glue gun, two 1½" dia. ball-shaped wooden turnings, 30" length of 1" dia. dowel, and wood-tone spray.

1. Cut a 7½" square template from stencil plastic. With pocket centered, draw around template on shirt. Cut one square pocket piece from each shirt. Press raw edges of each square ¼" to wrong side.
2. Arrange pocket pieces on background fabric; topstitch squares along pressed edges.
3. Press top edge of background and one edge of backing piece ½" to wrong side. Matching right sides and raw edges, and leaving pressed edges open, use a ½" seam allowance to sew background and backing pieces together. Trim corners, turn right side out, and press.
4. Cut six cuffs from shirts; trim loose threads. Move buttons if necessary so that all cuffs, when buttoned, are the same diameter. Button cuffs and flatten. Placing between background and backing, space cuffs evenly along top of wall hanging. Topstitch along top edge, catching cuffs in stitching.
5. For hanger, glue turnings to ends of dowel. Apply wood-tone spray to hanger; allow to dry. Slide hanger through cuffs.

a fresh approach

bring a sunny look to your outdoor décor with delightful decorations created from old cans, teacups, bottles, broken dinnerware, and other "recycled" items. You'll be proud to display an eye-catching gazing globe, patio lights, dressed-up terra-cotta candleholders, attractive concrete garden ornaments, a doll cradle flower bed, and more — all cleverly crafted from things you would ordinarily throw away!

ROCK-A-BYE FLOWER BED

Even your most delicate blooms will "rock" when planted in this restored doll cradle! Beverage and tuna cans cut and painted to resemble pretty posies add a playful splash of color to the flower bed.

DOLL CRADLE PLANTER

Recycled items: wooden doll cradle, three 1½"h x 3¼" dia. (tuna) cans, and three 12-oz. aluminum beverage cans

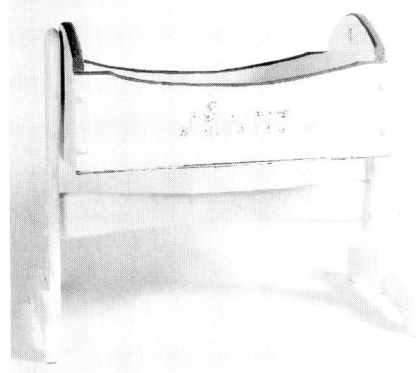

You will also need sand paper; tack cloth; white spray primer; white, ecru, yellow, pink, and green acrylic paint; paintbrushes; tin snips; tracing paper; household cement; and clear acrylic spray sealer.

Allow primer, paint, glue, and sealer to dry after each application.

1. If necessary, sand cradle; wipe with tack cloth.
2. Apply primer, then two coats of white paint to cradle; add green edges, if desired.
3. For each flower, use tin snips to cut 3¼" dia. can from top rim to bottom rim; cut away and discard top rim. To make petals, cut down sides of can at 1¼" intervals; round off corners. Bend petals outward.
4. For each flower center, cut through opening and down side of beverage can; cut away and discard top. Cut around can ½" from bottom; set aside upper piece for leaves. Cut down sides of can bottom at ¼" intervals to make fringe; bend fringe outward.
5. Trace leaf pattern, page 149, onto tracing paper; cut out. Use pattern to cut four leaves from reserved can pieces. Fold leaves lengthwise to form crease; unfold.
6. Apply primer to flowers and leaves. Paint leaves green, flowers yellow, and centers ecru with pink fringe. Glue centers to flowers; glue leaves around flowers. Glue flowers to side of cradle. Paint green tendrils around flowers.
7. Apply two coats of sealer to planter.

Butterfly "De-lights"

Add a touch of whimsy to your next backyard barbecue with a fun string of butterfly lights. Children will especially enjoy watching them flutter fancy-free around the patio all evening!

Butterfly Patio Lights

Recycled items: 12-oz. aluminum beverage cans and a strand of Christmas lights

You will also need utility scissors, tracing paper, spray primer, desired colors of acrylic paint, paintbrushes, clear acrylic spray sealer, hammer, nail, household cement, heavy-gauge silver craft wire, wire cutters, and a pencil.

Allow primer, paint, sealer, and household cement to dry after each application.

1. For each butterfly, use utility scissors to cut through hole in beverage can down to bottom rim of can. Cut away and discard top and bottom of can; flatten can piece.
2. Trace wing and body patterns, page 154, onto tracing paper; cut out. Draw around patterns on can pieces; cut out shapes.
3. Apply primer to both sides of shapes, then paint as desired. Apply two to three coats of sealer.
4. Arrange body on wings. Gently bend shapes in half lengthwise. Use hammer and nail to punch two small holes through body and wings to attach antennae.
5. Aligning holes, use household cement to glue body to wings. Fold a 6" length of wire in half; loosely thread wire from underside of wings through body. Place socket of one light through loop in wire; pull wire until light is tight against wings. Curl wire ends around pencil.

PERKY PLANT HANG-UPS

It's fun and easy to dress up the garden gate (or a plain old fence) with these sunny hanging plant holders! Save your empty coffee cans and perk them up with thumb-painted flowers.

COFFEE CAN PLANT HOLDERS

Recycled items: one-pound coffee cans

For each plant holder, you will also need a metal over-the-door wreath hanger, can opener, welding compound, spray primer, desired color spray paint for plant holder, desired colors of acrylic paint for flowers, paper towels, paintbrush, and clear spray sealer.

Allow welding compound, primer, paint, and sealer to dry after each application.

1. Straighten round end of hanger. Use can opener to cut an opening in front bottom of can large enough to insert end of hanger. Bend straightened end of hanger 1" and place in hole, then shape hanger across bottom and up side of can (Fig. 1). Follow welding compound manufacturer's instructions to "weld" hanger to can.

Fig. 1

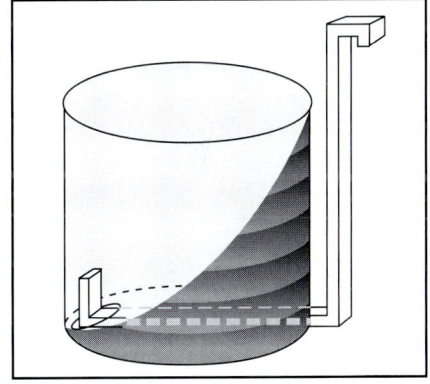

2. Apply primer, then spray paint plant holder.
3. For each flower petal, dip pad of thumb in desired color of acrylic paint; lightly blot on paper towel. Reapplying paint to thumb as necessary, make desired number of flowers on plant holder.
4. Use paintbrush to paint stems and leaves for each flower and tip of paintbrush handle to add dots to each flower. Apply sealer to plant holder.

Chill Out

Romantic evenings under the stars or lazy summer afternoons with friends will be more pleasant with this standing ice bucket on the patio. A large metal pot perched on a stool frame provides a convenient and decorative way to keep drinks chilly.

Patio Ice Bucket

Recycled items: large pot with lid (we used a canning pot) and a frame from a metal stool large enough to accommodate pot

You will also need sandpaper, tack cloth, welding compound, spray primer, and blue hammered-metal-finish spray paint.

1. Remove seat from stool; discard.
2. Use sandpaper to remove any rust on pot and stool frame; wipe with tack cloth.
3. Follow manufacturer's instructions to "weld" pot to stool frame.
4. Apply primer to outside of ice bucket and lid and allow to dry. Paint outside of ice bucket and lid blue; allow to dry.

LOVELY ILLUMINATION

*B*ring creative ambience to your next garden party with this unique candleholder. Salvage a leftover brick and plastic lids from spray bottles, add a touch of paint, tuck in a few flowers, and you've built a lovely illuminator!

BRICK VOTIVE HOLDER

Recycled items: four plastic caps (we used caps from hair spray bottles), rectangular lid from tin large enough to accommodate brick, brick with five holes, and several silk flowers with leaves

You will also need household cement, gold spray paint, gold and green acrylic paint, household sponges, aluminum foil, three green taper candles, and a hot glue gun.

Refer to Painting Techniques, page 157, before beginning project. Allow cement and paint to dry after each application.

1. For base, use cement to attach plastic caps to top of lid for legs. Spray paint base gold.
2. *Sponge Paint* brick green, then gold. Place brick on base.
3. Crumple a piece of foil around base of each candle. Hot glue candles in center and outer holes in brick.
4. Arrange flowers in remaining holes; hot glue to secure.

CANDLELIGHT DINING

Stop scratchin' around for something fancy to cradle votives. Instead, craft this clever candleholder using a chicken feeder and clay saucers. Painted and whitewashed, then filled with sand and shells, the unique candelabra will brighten any room with seaside flair.

CHICKEN FEEDER CANDLEHOLDER

Recycled items: 6" dia. metal chicken feeder, one small and one large clay saucer (we used 6" and 12" dia. saucers), sand, and assorted seashells

You will also need spray primer, white and terra-cotta acrylic paint, paintbrushes, clear acrylic spray sealer, three votive candles, and one pillar candle.

Refer to Painting Techniques, page 157, before beginning project. Allow primer, paint, and sealer to dry after each application.

1. Apply primer, then two coats of terra-cotta paint to chicken feeder.
2. *Dry Brush* feeder and saucers with white paint, then apply two to three coats of sealer.
3. Fill bottom of feeder and large saucer with sand. Place small saucer upside down in large saucer, then chicken feeder on small saucer.
4. Arrange shells, votives, and candle on candleholder.

SPORTY GARDEN SCULPTURES

These smooth stones will give a new look to any budding flower bed. They're a cinch to make — simply fill old hollow balls, such as basketballs, with mortar, allow to harden, and then cut and peel away the ball covering.

CONCRETE GARDEN ORNAMENTS

Recycled items: gallon plastic milk jug and hollow balls in assorted sizes (we used a basketball, mini basketball, and small rubber ball)

You will also need a utility knife, ready-to-use mortar mix, bucket, and sandpaper.

1. Cut milk jug in half; use top half for funnel and bottom half for scoop.
2. Use utility knife to cut a hole in each ball large enough to insert funnel.
3. For each ornament, follow manufacturer's instructions to mix mortar; use scoop to fill ball with mortar. Lightly tap ball to remove any air bubbles. Let mortar set for 24 to 48 hours or until hardened.
4. Use utility knife to cut ball away from mortar. If necessary, use sandpaper to smooth ornament.

DANCING DRAGONFLY

This delightful dragonfly will dance in the warm summer breezes. A length of copper pipe forms its body, and a scrap of screen wire serves as its jeweled, gossamer wings.

COPPER DRAGONFLY

Recycled items: 1" dia. copper pipe, aluminum window screen, and two aluminum beverage can pull tabs

You will also need a hack saw, hot glue gun, 1" dia. copper coupler, hammer, copper wire, wire cutters, utility scissors, and $1/2$" dia. gold cabochons.

1. For body, cut one 13" length from pipe. For head, glue coupler to one end of body. Use hammer to flatten opposite end of body.
2. For legs, twist two 10" lengths of wire together. Wrap wire around body $4^{1}/_{2}$" from head; twist to secure and coil ends to form feet.
3. For wings, cut a 12" x 24" piece from screen. Fanfold wings between short edges; wrap wire around gathers to secure. Place wings on body; wrap and crisscross wire around gathers and body to hold wings in place.
4. Glue pull tabs, then cabochons to head for eyes. Glue remaining cabochons to wings, as desired.

GAZING GLOBE

Do you see a gazing globe in the future of your backyard? This lovely addition to any garden comes together simply by painting a glass light fixture and securing it atop a tall candleholder.

GAZING GLOBE

Recycled items: glass light globe with globe mounting bracket and screws and a metal pillar candleholder

You will also need grey spray primer, chrome and black spray paint, and welding compound.

Allow primer, paint, and welding compound to dry after each application.

1. Apply primer to globe, bracket, screws, and candleholder. Apply two to three coats of chrome paint to globe.
2. For stand, follow manufacturer's instructions to "weld" bracket to candleholder.
3. Paint stand and screws black.
4. Place globe on stand upside down; secure in bracket with screws.

Tiered Terra-Cotta

*S*ow the seeds of your creativity in this unusual tiered planter. Your garden will spring to life in this eye-catching arrangement of terra-cotta saucers and flowerpots.

Tiered Planter

Recycled items: two clay garden dishes and three clay flowerpots (we used 12" dia. x 2¼"h and 8¾" dia. x 3½"h garden dishes and 3½" dia. x 3½"h, 2¾" dia. x 3"h, and 4½" dia. x 3½"h flowerpots)

You will also need household cement.

Use cement for all gluing. Allow cement to dry after each application.

1. Beginning with larger garden dish, stack and glue upside-down flowerpot, smaller garden dish, second upside-down flowerpot, then right side-up flowerpot at center of larger garden dish to form planter.
2. Fill planter with your favorite plants.

FLUTTERING FANCIES

Capture warm summer breezes with these fanciful windsocks! To create the fluttering streamers, tear an assortment of strips from pretty fabric scraps and paint a tiny clay pot to match. We chose soft colors for a feminine look, but you could also use bright colors to make livelier accents.

FLOWERPOT WINDSOCKS

Recycled item: fabric scraps

You will also need acrylic paint, paintbrushes, clay flowerpots (we used 1", 1$^1/_2$", and 2" dia. flowerpots), and a black permanent fine point marker.

Refer to Painting Techniques, page 157, before beginning project. Allow paint to dry after each application.

1. For each windsock, paint flowerpot as desired; use marker to outline details.
2. Tear desired number of $^5/_8$" x 14" fabric strips for streamers. Tear one $^5/_8$" x 20" fabric strip for hanger.
3. Place streamers together; knot hanger around center of bundle.
4. From inside of pot, thread hanger through hole in bottom of pot; knot ends together. Trim streamers if desired.

Terra-cotta Candleholder

The flame of creativity burns bright with this project. Two terra-cotta saucers of different sizes, with bottoms glued together, form a nice resting place for a large candle.

Terra-cotta Candleholder

Recycled items: two terra-cotta saucers (we used one 6" and one 7" dia. saucer)

You will also need clear paintable silicone caulk, spray primer, assorted acrylic paint, paintbrushes, and clear acrylic spray sealer.

Refer to Painting Techniques and Dots, page 157, before beginning project. Allow caulk, primer, paint, and sealer to dry after each application.

1. Use caulk to glue bottoms of saucers together.
2. Apply a thin ring of caulk around saucers where bottoms meet. Apply primer to candleholder; paint candleholder as desired.
3. Apply two to three coats of sealer to candleholder.

STENCILED SETTINGS

You'll be floored by the simplicity of this giant table-size place mat! A remnant of vinyl flooring will create a generous, durable canvas for you to stencil fun place settings ready for any table, any meal!

STENCILED TABLE TOPPER

Recycled items: piece of vinyl flooring to cover patio table and cardboard

You will also need utility scissors; white gesso; paintbrushes; drawing compass; yellow, blue, dark blue, grey, and silver acrylic paint; stencil brushes; paintbrushes; stencil plastic; craft knife and cutting mat; and clear waterproof sealer.

Refer to Stenciling and Painting Techniques, page 157, before beginning project. Allow gesso, paint, and sealer to dry after each application.

1. Use utility scissors to cut a piece of vinyl to fit tabletop.
2. Apply three coats of gesso to wrong side of vinyl.
3. Use compass to draw one 7" dia. plate pattern on cardboard; cut out. Using pattern, draw four plates on topper; paint plates blue. Use compass to draw one 5" dia. bottom circle at center on plate pattern; cut out. Draw around bottom circle on each plate; paint over circle with dark blue. Paint yellow and dark blue details on plates.
4. Trace napkin and silverware patterns, page 150, onto stencil plastic; cut out leaving outer plastic uncut. Stencil one yellow napkin beside each plate. Using blue and dark blue paint, paint details on napkins. Stencil one silver fork, knife, and spoon at each place setting; outline utensils grey.
6. Apply four coats of sealer to vinyl.

Floating Candlelight

Placed in a garden pond or swimming pool, this floating blossom provides a mood-setting glow. The votive candleholder is formed from gallon-size plastic bottles and a yellow plastic-foam food tray. Buttons glued to the center give this project its cheery daisy appeal.

Floating Candleholder

Recycled items: two one-gallon bleach bottles, yellow plastic foam food tray, and four plastic sewing spools the same size

You will also need utility scissors, tracing paper, black permanent fine-point marker, hot glue gun, votive candleholder, and votive candle.

1. Use utility scissors to cut away tops from bottles just under handles. For flower center, draw around cut end of one bottle on food tray; set aside.
2. Draw a line around bottles 2" from bottom. Trace petal pattern, page 147, onto tracing paper; cut out. Place narrow end of pattern along drawn line; use marker to draw around pattern. Repeat pattern around both bottles (Fig. 1).

Cut out petals along drawn lines; cut areas between bottoms of petals will form points.

Fig. 1

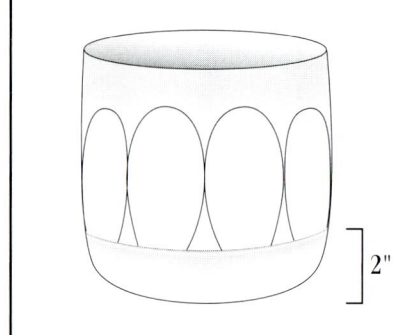

3. Bend petals and points outward. Staggering petals, stack and glue flowers together.
4. Cut out flower center. Draw around bottom of votive holder at center of flower center; cut out circle.
5. Glue spools to bottom of flower center. Glue flower center in flower; glue buttons on center.
6. Place votive holder, then candle in hole in center of flower.

CANDLELIGHT TOWERS

It's perfectly clear — instead of tossing your mismatched tumblers into the rummage sale box, you should use them to craft colorful candleholders! Stack and cement glasses as desired; then paint with freehand designs to suit your style.

DRINKING-GLASS CANDLEHOLDERS

Recycled items: assorted clear drinking glasses

You will also need clear-drying household cement, rubbing alcohol, cotton balls, desired colors of glass paint, paintbrushes, and clear acrylic spray sealer.

Refer to Painting Techniques, page 157, before beginning project. Allow household cement, paint, and sealer to dry after each application.

1. Use household cement to glue bottoms of glasses together.
2. Clean glasses with alcohol. Paint candleholders as desired.
3. Apply two to three coats of sealer to candleholders.

Garden Elegance

This elegant planter looks like it's carved from granite, but it's easy and inexpensive to craft using a cardboard mailing tube and textured spray paint. Display it in a sheltered area for a refined focal point.

Plant Pedestal

Recycled items: two plastic bowls, round wooden platter, and a cardboard mailing tube with end caps

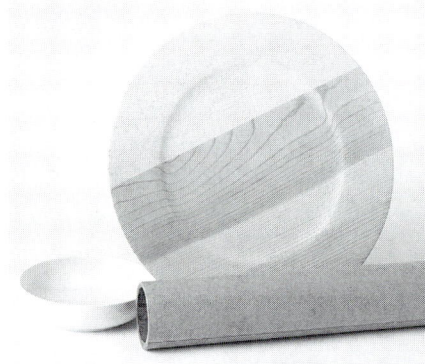

You will also need sandpaper, tack cloth, household cement, spray primer, and textured spray paint.

Allow cement, primer, and spray paint to dry after each application.

1. Lightly sand bowls and platter; wipe with tack cloth.
2. Center and cement one bowl upside down on bottom of platter, glue tube on bowl, and remaining bowl right side up on top of tube.
3. Apply primer to pedestal. Follow manufacturer's instructions to apply textured paint to pedestal.

"INVISIBLE" PLANTER

Your prized flowers will be the star of the show with this almost-invisible planter! Bring those old tomato cages out of the garden shed to fashion the frame and use chicken wire to form the moss-lined baskets.

TOMATO CAGE PLANTER

Recycled item: tomato cage

You will also need pliers, wire cutters, chicken wire, sheet moss, and desired plants.

1. Place cage upside down. Use pliers to form a loop in end of each stake.
2. Measure diameter of top ring of cage; multiply by two. Using the determined diameter, use wire cutters to cut a circle from chicken wire. Form circle into a bowl to fit in top ring of cage. Use pliers to wrap cut ends of wire bowl around ring to secure. Repeat for remaining rings on cage.
3. Line each bowl with moss, then fill bowls with plants.

FENCE-RAIL FLAG

Add a touch of Americana to the backyard with this rustic flag. Paint garden stakes red and white to form the stripes and cut the gleaming stars from flattened beverage cans.

FENCE POST FLAG

Recycled items: five aluminum beverage cans

You will also need white, red, and blue acrylic paint; paintbrushes; eight 36" long wooden stakes; 9½" x 16½" piece of ⅜" plywood; saw; small nails; hammer; wood-tone spray; utility scissors; and tracing paper.

Allow paint and wood-tone spray to dry after each application.

1. Paint five stakes white, three stakes red, and plywood blue. Cut one white stake in half for vertical supports.
2. For flag, arrange stakes on supports; nail in place. Position plywood on flag; nail in place.
3. Lightly apply wood-tone spray to flag.
4. Use utility scissors to cut through opening of each can to bottom rim; cut away and discard top and bottom.
5. Trace star pattern, page 146, onto tracing paper; cut out. Use pattern to cut fifteen stars from can pieces. Arrange stars on flag and nail in place.

Garden Candle Shield

Enjoying a breezy summer evening on the patio is even nicer by candlelight, and with this shielded holder you don't have to worry about flickering or smoking candles. We cut up an aluminum can to create our painted shield.

SHIELDED CANDLEHOLDER

Recycled items: 24-oz. aluminum beverage can and a 2½" dia. x 3" tall glass jar

You will also need white spray primer; tracing paper; transfer paper; clear removable tape; stylus or sharp pencil; craft knife or small sharp utility scissors; yellow, red, light green, green, and dark green acrylic paint; assorted paintbrushes; cosmetic sponges; clear spray sealer; sand; and wood glue.

Refer to Painting Techniques, page 157, before beginning project. Allow primer, paint, and sealer to dry after each application.

1. Apply primer to can. Trace tree pattern, page 146, onto tracing paper. Tape transfer paper, then pattern ¾" from bottom of can. Use stylus to draw over pattern. Use craft knife or small scissors to cut can along drawn lines and around bottom of can for candleholder.
2. Paint candleholder green. Lightly *Sponge Paint* base, tree and bushes dark green. Use sponge to add light green highlights to base, trunk of tree, top of tree, and tops of bushes. Paint thin dark green blades of grass on base, red apples on tree, and yellow highlights on some apples and bushes. Apply sealer to candleholder.
3. To secure jar in candleholder, mix three tablespoons of sand with two tablespoons of wood glue. Add green paint to sand mixture until desired color is achieved. Fill base of candleholder with sand mixture. Center jar in sand mixture. Allow to dry 24 hours.

Chairback Planter

Salvage the back of a worn-out chair to create this unique planter. It's perfect for pampering a plant that needs room to grow.

Ladder-Back Chair Planter

Recycled items: ladder-back chair and an oval galvanized tub large enough to accommodate width of chair back

You will also need a saw, sandpaper, tack cloth, spray primer, desired colors of acrylic paint, paintbrushes, motifs cut from wrapping paper, decoupage glue, foam brush, clear matte spray sealer, crackle medium, clear varnish, frosted glazing medium, drill and bits, and four 1" long wood screws.

Allow primer, paint, decoupage glue, sealer, varnish, and glaze to dry after each application.

1. Cut back from chair just above seat.
2. Sand chair back and tub with tack cloth; apply primer, then desired color paint.
3. Follow *Decoupage*, page 157, to apply motifs to tub and chair rungs; then seal tub and chair rungs. 
4. Follow manufacturer's instructions to apply crackle medium to tub and chair rungs, using varnish as a topcoat.
5. Mix two parts glaze medium with one part desired color paint. Apply a thin layer of glaze mixture to tub and chairback.
6. Center chairback at back of tub. Drill pilot holes through tub and uprights, then use screws to attach chairback to tub.

GREAT SERVING CRATE

SODA CRATE SERVING TRAY

This serving tray is more than just "soda" great ... it's accessible, handy, and eye-pleasing! The simple caddy — made by repainting an old-time wooden soda crate, some bottle caps, and round legs — will be a colorful, fun addition at any outing.

Recycled items: wooden soda crate and three metal bottle caps

You will also need masking tape; spray primer; white, ivory, yellow, dark yellow, light green, green, and black acrylic paint; assorted paintbrushes; 1/2" dia. foam brush; four 3" high wooden finials for legs; hammer; small nails; wood glue; and clear acrylic spray sealer.

Refer to Painting Techniques, page 157, before beginning project. Allow primer, paint, and sealer to dry after each application.

1. If necessary, use tape to mask metal portions of crate. Apply primer, then two coats of yellow paint to crate. Paint black and white checkerboards along top long edges. Use round foam brush to paint ivory dots on sides of crate. Paint legs light green; paint green spirals around each leg.

2. Paint leaf and vine designs on front of crate.

3. Use hammer to flatten bottle caps. Apply primer to caps, then paint yellow. Paint a dark yellow swirl on each cap. Nail caps to front of crate. Paint nail heads ivory.

4. If necessary, remove tape from crate. Glue one leg to crate at each bottom corner. Apply two to three coats of sealer to crate and legs.

Canister Topiary

A potted wreath of ivy provides an attractive table accent. The base is a pleasantly painted coffee can, and the wreath is shaped from a coat hanger covered in ivy garland.

Coffee Can Topiary

Recycled items: large coffee can and a coat hanger

You will also need spray primer, assorted acrylic paint, paintbrushes, clear acrylic spray sealer, floral foam, craft glue, sheet moss, artificial ivy garland, and green floral wire.

Allow primer, paint, and sealer to dry after each application.

1. Apply primer to can. Paint can as desired; apply two to three coats of sealer.
2. Fill can to 1" from top with foam. Glue moss over foam.
3. Straighten hook on coat hanger. Shape coat hanger into a circle. Apply glue to straightened hook and insert into foam.
4. Arrange garland around coat hanger; wire in place.

Dresser-Drawer Planter

*Y*ou'll receive a drawerful of compliments when you feature your favorite blossoms in this perky planter. Attach table legs, apply paint, and decoupage seed packet motifs on the front to complete the disguise.

Drawer Planter

Recycled items: two wooden drawers the same size

You will also need wood glue; furniture clamps; drill and bits; four 1" long bolts with nuts; 1/2" plywood; four leg mounting brackets; four wooden table legs; spray primer; white, yellow, orange, and black acrylic paint; paintbrushes; natural sponges; soft cloth; decoupage glue; motifs from flower seed wrapping paper or packets; and clear acrylic spray sealer.

Allow glues, primer, paint, and sealer to dry after each application.

1. Aligning backs of drawers, use wood glue to glue drawers together; use furniture clamps to hold in place until dry. Drilling a pilot hole first, insert one bolt at each corner of drawer backs to secure.
2. Measure width and length of bottom of drawers; cut a piece from plywood the determined measurements. Use wood glue to glue plywood piece in place.
3. Attach one mounting bracket at each bottom corner of planter; twist legs into brackets.
4. Apply primer, then two coats of yellow paint to planter. For wash, mix one part water with two parts orange paint; use sponge to apply wash over planter, then wipe off immediately with soft cloth. Paint black and white checkerboards around legs as desired.
5. Follow *Decoupage*, page 157, to apply motifs on front of planter.
6. Apply two to three coats of sealer to planter.

PERCOLATED POSY

*B*looming with pizzazz, this snazzy tin flower will be a highlight for any flower bed. Simple instructions take you through cutting and "tin-ting" techniques, making this budding beauty a success for the crafty gardener.

PERCOLATED POSY

Recycled items: 6 1/8" dia. x 6 3/4" high coffee can and four 12-oz. beverage cans

You will also need tracing paper; tin snips; hammer; awl; utility scissors; wooden pencil; crimping tool; white spray primer; 24" of 1" dia. PVC pipe for stem; 1" dia. washer; pink spray paint; yellow, pink, dark pink, and green acrylic paint; paintbrushes; pipe cap to fit PVC pipe; drill with 1/16" drill bit; one 2" long wood screw; hot glue gun; and three 1/2" long sheet metal screws.

Wear heavy gloves and eye protection while cutting cans. Allow primer, paint, and sealer to dry after each application.

1. Mark side of can at 2¾" intervals.
2. Trace petal and leaf patterns, page 152, onto tracing paper; cut out. Referring to Fig. 1, use pattern to draw petals on can. Use tin snips to cut along drawn lines; leave points between petal bottoms (sepals) attached to bottom of can. Bend petals and sepals outward.

Fig. 1

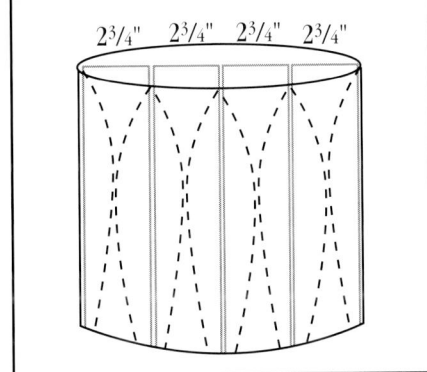

3. Twist each petal slightly in the same direction. Use hammer and awl to punch one hole at center bottom of flower.
4. For pistil, draw a line 3½" from bottom of one beverage can. Cut on line; discard top. Make 1" long cuts 1" apart around top edge of can; round corners to make small petals. Roll petals outward around pencil. Punch hole at center bottom of pistil.
5. Cutting through openings in remaining beverage cans, cut down each can to bottom rim; cut away and discard tops and bottoms of cans. Flatten remaining pieces. Use pattern to cut three leaves from pieces. Use crimping tool to crimp each leaf.
6. Apply primer to both sides of flower, pistil, leaves, washer, and pipe stem.
7. Spray both sides of flower pink. Paint inside of pistil dark pink; paint outside of pistil, stem, washer, pipe cap, and sepals green. Paint additional details on flower as desired.
8. Drill a hole 2½" from one end of stem; fill with hot glue. To assemble flower, place washer, pistil, then flower on a wood screw. Insert screw in hole in stem. Place pipe cap on top of stem.
9. Glue one end of each leaf to stem. Drill through glued part of each leaf into stem; add sheet metal screw to secure. Paint screw heads green.

Garden Beauties

Spruce up a garden nook with an inviting gate and soothing striped bench. Transformed by a little paint, the secondhand pieces offer a picturesque place for you to savor nature's wonders.

GARDEN GATE AND BENCH

Recycled items: metal chain-link gate and wooden bench

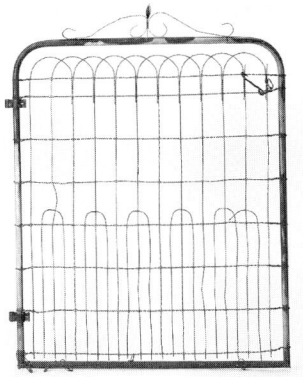

You will also need sandpaper; tack cloth; spray primer; ivory spray paint; ivory, yellow, and green acrylic paint; paintbrushes; clear exterior spray sealer; and painter's masking tape.

Allow primer, paint, and sealer to dry after each application. Arrange finished gate and bench as desired.

GATE
1. If necessary, sand gate to remove rust; wipe with tack cloth.
2. Spray gate with primer then ivory paint.
3. Paint gate frame green. If gate has decorative scrollwork, paint green and yellow.
4. Apply two to three coats of sealer to gate.

BENCH
1. If necessary, sand bench; wipe with tack cloth. Use acrylic paint to paint bench ivory.
2. Use masking tape to evenly space and mask horizontal stripes on bench. Paint unmasked areas green; remove tape.
3. Use masking tape to evenly space and mask vertical stripes on bench. Paint unmasked areas green; remove tape.
4. Lightly sand bench except where stripes intersect and overlap; wipe with tack cloth.
5. Apply two to three coats of sealer to bench.

Patterns

FLOATING CANDLEHOLDER
(page 132)

BABY WALL QUILT
(page 106)

CHEST KITCHEN CART
(page 9)

147

PATTERNS (continued)

Color Key

- yellow
- light pink
- medium pink
- dark pink
- light green
- dark green
- brown

Stitch Key

Stitch Name	Symbol
French Knot	●
Lazy Daisy	○
Running Stitch	- - -
Straight Stitch	—
Chain Stitch	⚬⚬⚬
Blanket Stitch	⊥

SOCK APPLIQUÉ PILLOW
(page 105)

Bloom where you're planted!

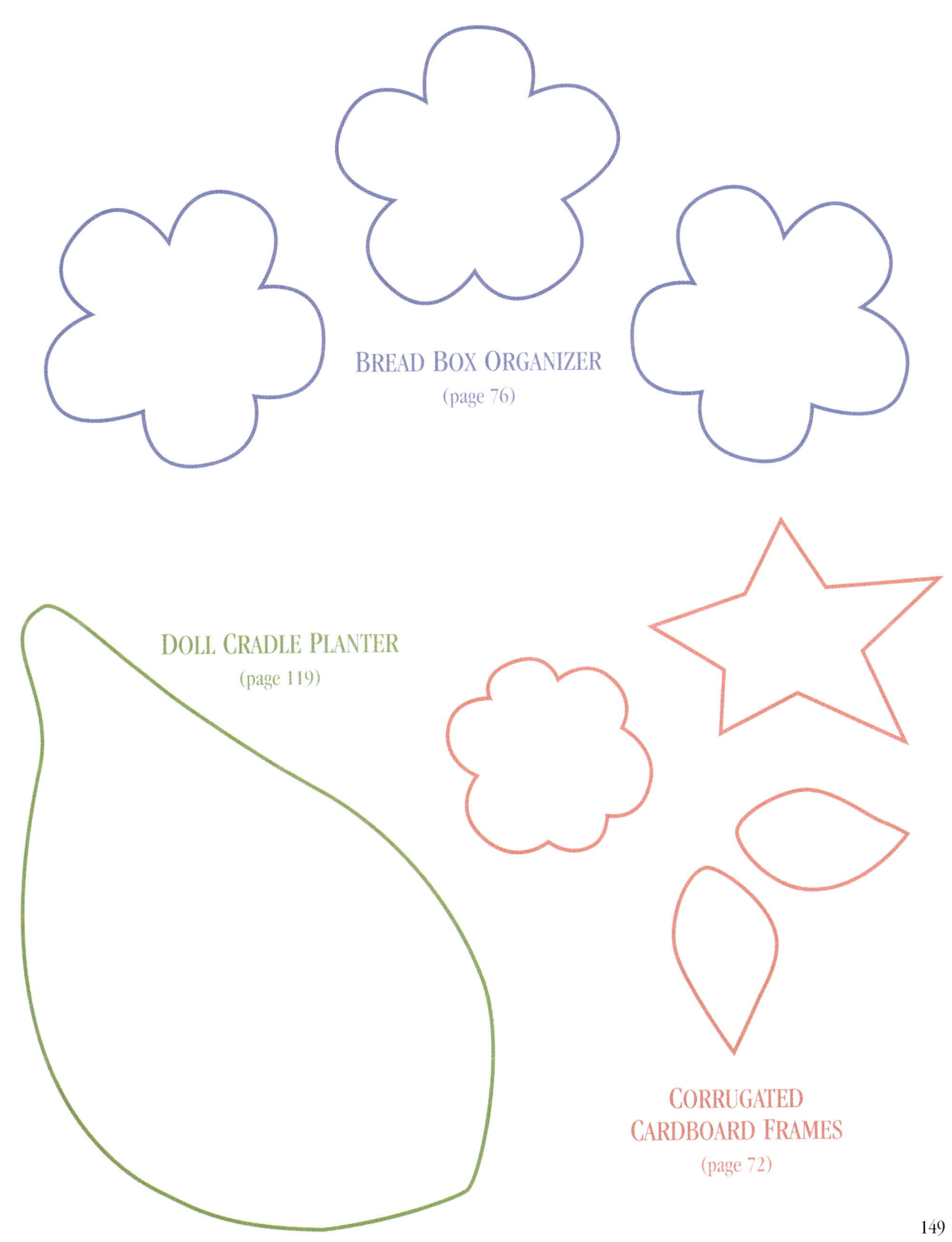

PATTERNS (continued)

STENCILED TABLE SETTING
(page 131)

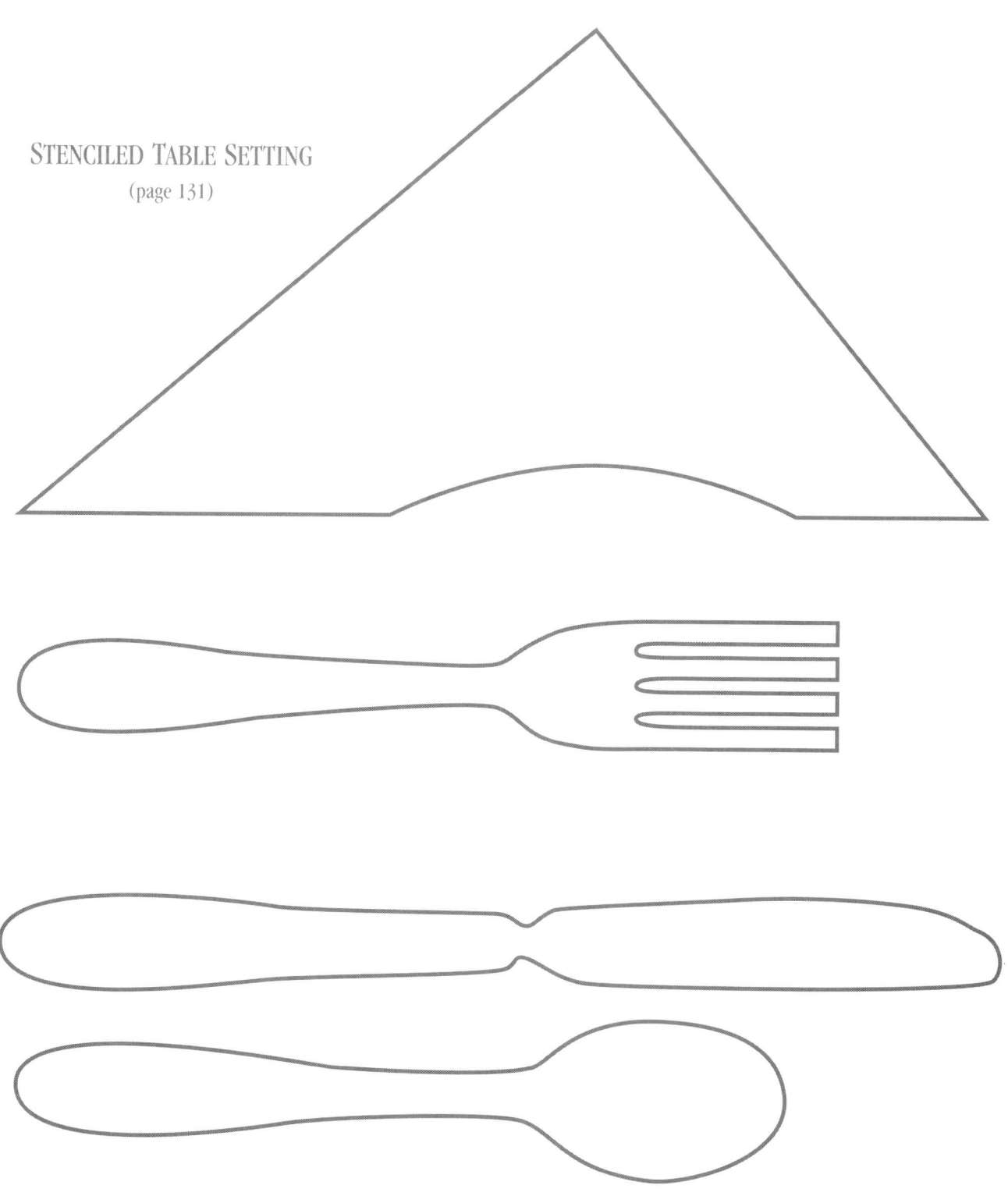

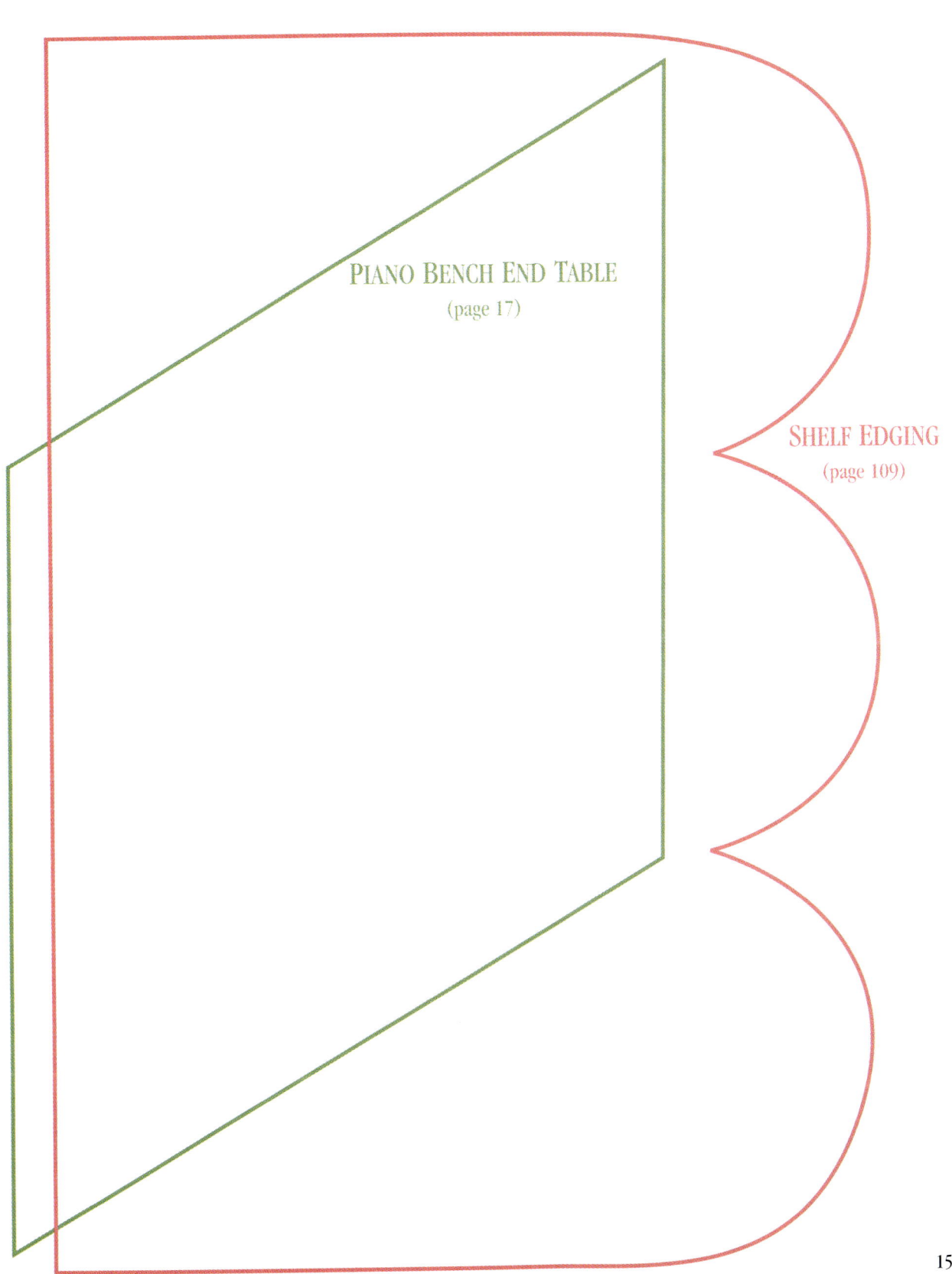

PATTERNS (continued)

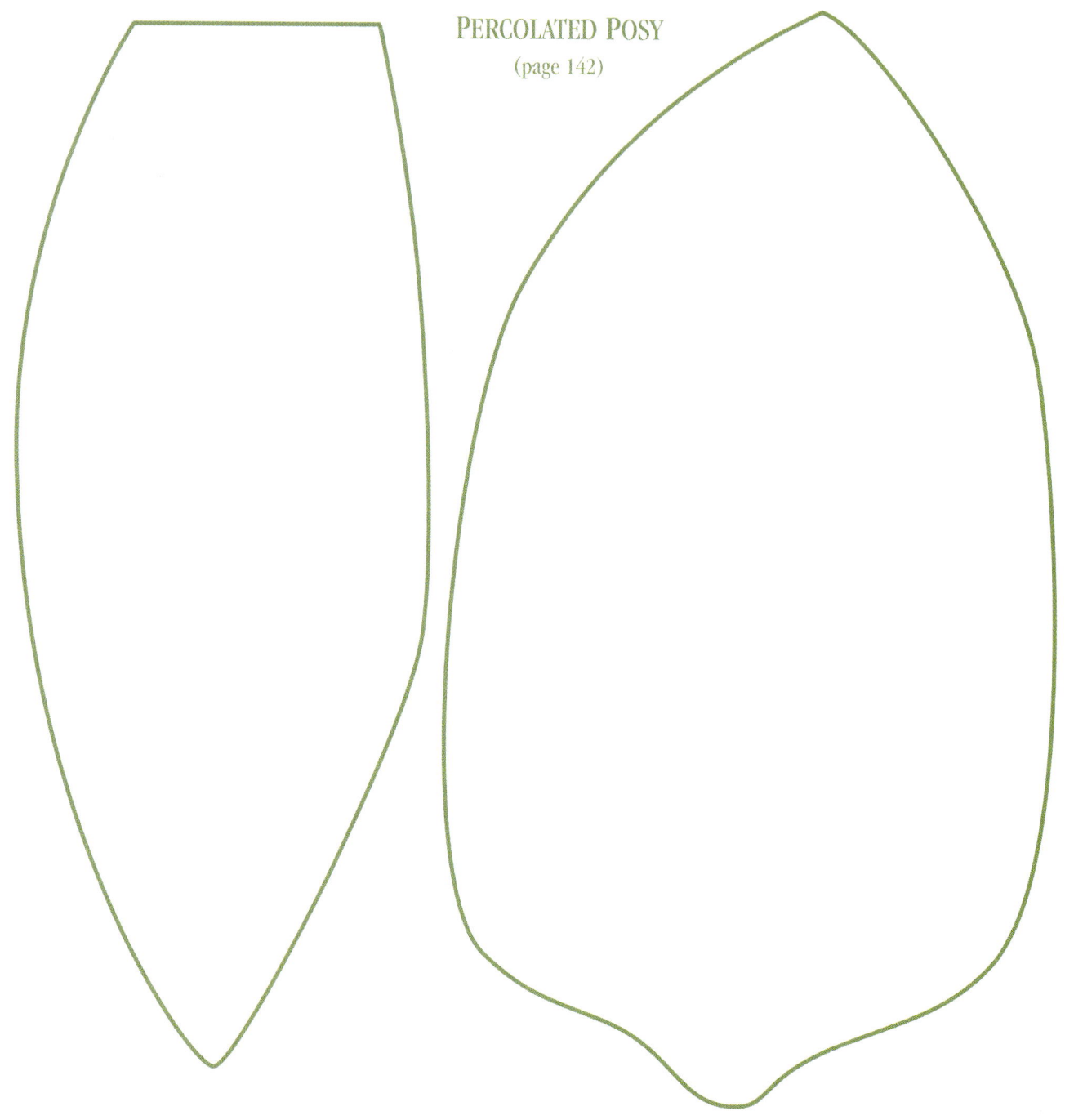

PERCOLATED POSY
(page 142)

CABINET DOOR
MESSAGE CENTER
(page 79)

PATTERNS (continued)

BUTTERFLY PATIO LIGHTS (page 120)

BEVERAGE CAN FRAME (page 89)

EGGSHELL MOSAIC
(page 55)

LIGHTED CABIN
(page 71)

DIAGRAM

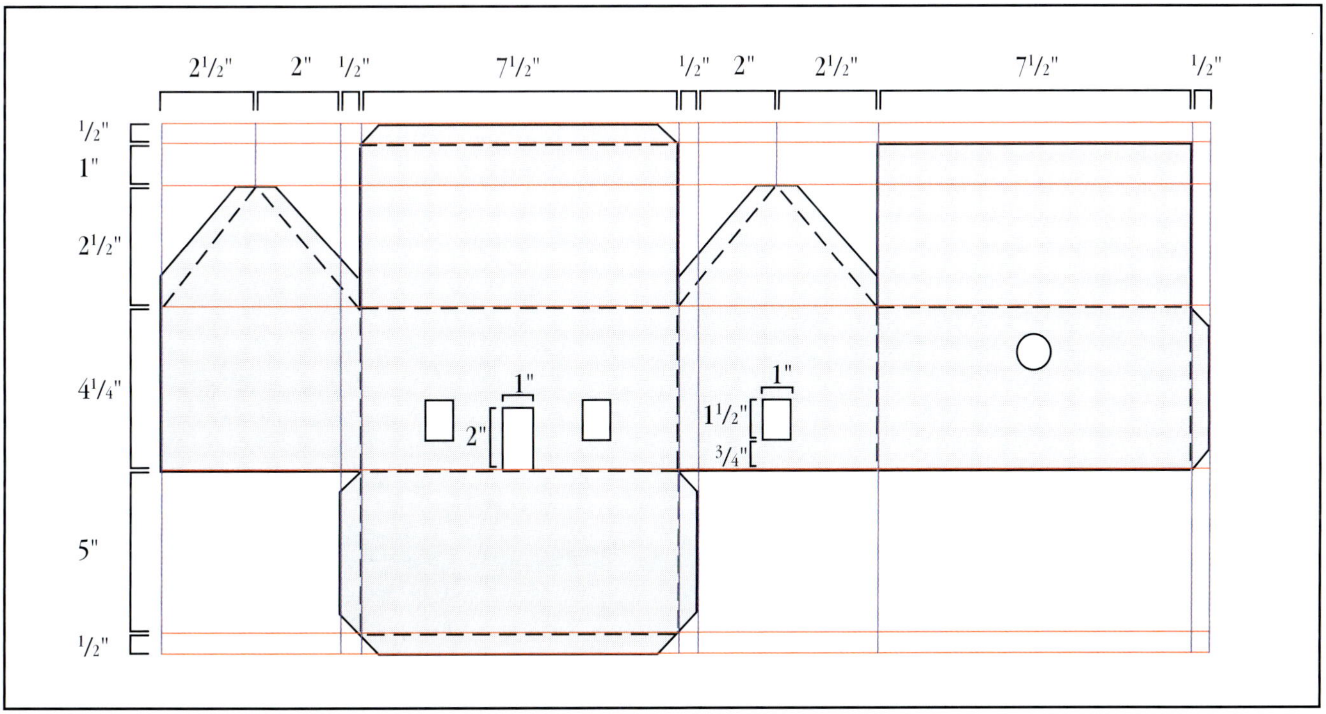

GENERAL INSTRUCTIONS

ADHESIVES

When using any adhesive, carefully follow the manufacturer's instructions.

White craft glue: Recommended for paper. Dry flat.

Tacky craft glue: Recommended for paper, fabric, florals, or wood. Dry flat or secure items with clothespins or straight pins until glue is dry.

Craft glue stick: Recommended for paper or for gluing small, lightweight items to paper or other surfaces. Dry flat.

Fabric glue: Recommended for fabric or paper. Dry flat or secure items with clothespins or straight pins until glue is dry.

Decoupage glue: Recommended for decoupage fabric or paper to a surface such as wood or glass. Use purchased decoupage glue or mix one part craft glue with one part water.

Hot or low-temperature glue gun: Recommended for paper, fabric, florals, or wood. Hold in place until set.

Rubber cement: Recommended for paper and cardboard. May discolor photos; may discolor paper with age. Dry flat (dries very quickly).

Spray adhesive: Recommended for paper or fabric. Can be repositioned or permanent. Dry flat.

Household Cement: Recommended for ceramic or metal. Secure items with clothespins until glue is dry.

Wood Glue: Recommended for wood. Nail, screw, or clamp items together until glue is dry.

COFFEE DYEING

1. Dissolve two tablespoons instant coffee in two cups hot water; allow to cool.
2. Soak fabric pieces in coffee several minutes. Remove from coffee and allow to dry; press.

MAKING PATTERNS

Place tracing paper over pattern and trace pattern; cut out.

For a more durable pattern, use a permanent pen to trace pattern onto stencil plastic; cut out.

FUSIBLE APPLIQUÉS

To prevent darker fabrics from showing through, white or light-colored fabrics may need to be lined with fusible interfacing before applying paper-backed fusible web.

Follow all steps for each appliqué. When tracing patterns for more than one appliqué, leave at least 1" between shapes on web.

To make a reverse appliqué piece, trace pattern onto tracing paper; turn traced pattern over and continue to follow all steps using reversed pattern.

When an appliqué pattern contains shaded areas, trace along entire outer line for appliqué indicated in project instructions. Trace outer lines of shaded areas separately for additional appliqués indicated in project instructions.

Appliqués can be temporarily held in place by touching appliqués with tip of iron. If appliqués are not in desired position, lift and reposition.

1. Use a pencil to trace pattern onto paper side of web as many times as indicated in project instructions for a single fabric. Repeat for additional patterns and fabrics.
2. Follow manufacturer's instructions to fuse traced patterns to wrong side of fabrics. Do not remove paper backing.
3. Cut out appliqué pieces along traced lines. Remove paper backing.
4. Overlapping as necessary, arrange appliqués web side down on project.
5. Fuse appliqués in place.

MACHINE APPLIQUÉ

Unless otherwise indicated in project instructions, set sewing machine for a medium-width zigzag stitch with a short stitch length. When using nylon or metallic thread, use regular thread in bobbin.

1. Pin or baste a piece of stabilizer slightly larger than design to wrong side of background fabric under design.
2. Beginning on straight edge of appliqué if possible, position project under presser foot so that most of stitching will be on appliqué piece. Hold upper thread toward you and sew two or three stitches over thread to prevent raveling. Stitch over all exposed raw edges of appliqué and along detail lines as indicated in project instructions.
3. When stitching is complete, remove stabilizer. Pull loose threads to wrong side of fabric; knot and trim ends.

STENCILING

These instructions are written for multicolor stencils. For single-color stencils, make one stencil for entire design.

1. For first stencil, cut a piece from stencil plastic 1" larger than entire pattern. Center plastic over pattern and use a permanent pen to trace outlines of all areas of first color in stencil cutting key. For placement guidelines, outline remaining colored area using dashed lines. Using a new piece of plastic for each additional color in stencil cutting key, repeat for remaining stencils.
2. Place each plastic piece on cutting mat and use craft knife to cut out stencil along solid lines, making sure edges are smooth.
3. Hold or tape stencil in place. Using a clean, dry stencil brush or sponge piece, dip brush or sponge in paint. Remove excess paint on a paper towel. Brush or sponge should be almost dry to produce best results. Beginning at edge of cutout area, apply paint in a stamping motion over stencil. If desired, highlight or shade design by stamping a lighter or darker shade of paint in cutout area. Repeat until all areas of first stencil have been painted. Carefully remove stencil and allow paint to dry.
4. Using stencils in order indicated in color key and matching guidelines on stencils to previously stenciled area, repeat Step 3 for remaining stencils.

DECOUPAGE

1. Cut desired motifs from fabric or paper.
2. Apply decoupage glue to wrong sides of motifs.
3. Arrange motifs on project as desired, overlapping as necessary. Smooth in place and allow to dry.
4. Allowing to dry after each application, spray project with two to three coats of varnish.

HAND APPLIQUÉ

1. Leaving $1/2$" between shapes, draw around patterns on wrong side of fabric.
2. Cut out shapes $1/4$" outside drawn lines. Press edges of shapes $1/4$" to right side. Clip curves and points up to, but not through drawn lines. Arrange and pin appliqués on project.
3. Use Blind Stitches to sew edges of appliqués to project.

PAINTING TECHNIQUES

TRANSFERRING A PATTERN
Trace pattern onto tracing paper. Place transfer paper coated side down between project and traced pattern. Use removable tape to secure pattern to project. Use a pencil to transfer outlines of design to project (press lightly to avoid smudges and heavy lines that are difficult to cover). If necessary, use a soft eraser to remove any smudges.

PAINTING BASECOATS
A disposable foam plate makes a good palette.

Use a medium round brush for large areas and a small round brush for small areas. Do not overload brush. Allowing to dry between coats, apply several thin coats of paint to project.

"C" STROKE
Dip an angle or flat paintbrush in paint. Touch tip to surface, pulling brush to the left. Pull brush toward you while  applying pressure. When stroke is desired length, lift brush gradually while pulling to the right to form the tail of the stroke.

COMMA STROKE
Dip round brush into water; blot on paper towel. Dip brush into paint; touch brush tip to painting surface.  Apply slight pressure to brush to spread out brush hairs. Pull brush to the right or left in a curve. Gradually release pressure on brush to make tail of stroke.

DOTS
Dip handle end of paintbrush into paint; touch to painting surface.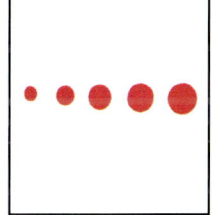

DOUBLE LOAD
Dip brush into water; blot on paper towel. Dip corner of brush into paint; dip the opposite corner of  brush into another shade of paint. Stroke brush on a palette or waxed paper to blend the two shades of paint.

GENERAL INSTRUCTIONS (continued)

DRY BRUSH
Do not dip brush in water. Dip a stipple brush or old paintbrush in paint; wipe most of the paint off onto a dry paper towel. Lightly rub the brush across the area to receive color. Decrease pressure on the brush as you move outward. Repeat as needed.

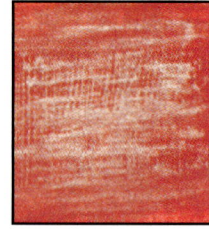

HIGHLIGHT
Select a paint that is lighter than the area you want to highlight. Dip flat brush into water; blot on paper towel. Dip corner of brush into paint; stroke brush on palette or waxed paper to blend. Stroke brush on area you wish to highlight.

LINE WORK
Mix paint with water to an ink-like consistency. Dip liner brush into thinned paint. Touch tip of brush to painting surface.

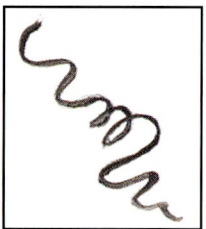

MARBLEIZING DETAILS
To create veins, drag a feather through vein paint color, then wiggle and flip feather as you drag it diagonally across surface.

SPONGE PAINTING
1. Dampen sponge with water.
2. Dip dampened sponge into paint; blot on paper towel to remove excess paint.
3. Use a light stamping motion to paint project.

TRANSFERRING DETAILS
To transfer detail lines to design, reposition pattern and transfer paper over painted base coats and use a pencil to lightly transfer detail lines onto project.

ADDING DETAILS
Use a permanent pen to draw over detail lines.

ROSEBUD
Paint colors: red, pink, white, and green

Double Load brush in red and pink. With pink on top, make a "C" Stroke for top of bud, then make a "C" Stroke for bottom of bud.

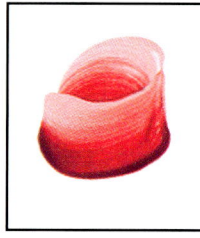

Use white to make Comma Strokes on top edges of bud. Use pink to make right and left Comma Strokes on either side of bud. Use green Line Work for leaves and stem.

LEAF #1
Paint colors: green and dark green.

Double Load brush. With dark green to outside, make an elongated "C" Stroke, wiggling brush to make ruffled edge of leaf. Repeat for opposite side of leaf.

Use green Line Work for center of leaf

LEAF #2
Paint colors: green and dark green

Double Load brush. With dark green to outside, make an elongated and curved "C" Stroke.

Use light green, then dark green Line Work for center of leaf.

EMBROIDERY STITCHES

BACKSTITCH
Bring needle up at 1; go down at 2. Bring needle up at 3 and back down at 1 (Fig. 1). Continue working to make a continuous line of stitches.

Fig. 1

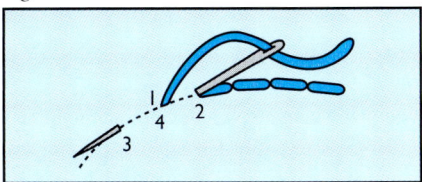

BLANKET STITCH
Bring needle up at 1; keeping thread below point of needle, go down at 2 and up at 3 (Fig. 2a). Continue working as shown in Fig. 2b.

Fig. 2a   Fig. 2b

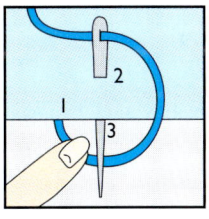 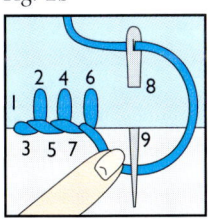

BLIND STITCH
Come up at 1. Go down at 2 and come up at 3 (Fig. 3). Length of stitches may be varied as desired.

Fig. 3

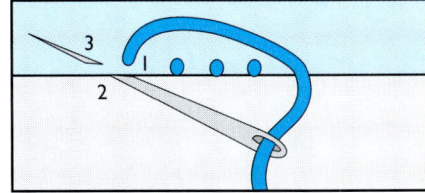

CHAIN STITCH
Bring needle up at 1 and down at 2, leaving a loop on top of fabric. Bring needle back up at 3 (Fig. 4a).

Go back down at 4 and up at 5 (Fig. 4b) to make another loop. End chain by bringing needle up through last loop and back down just outside of loop.

Fig. 4a   Fig. 4b

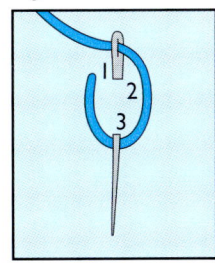 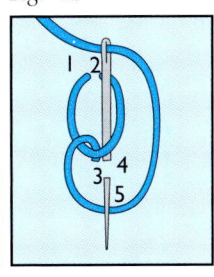

FRENCH KNOT
Bring needle up at 1. Wrap floss once around needle and insert needle at 2, holding floss with non-stitching fingers (Fig. 5). Tighten knot as close to fabric as possible while pulling needle back through fabric. For larger knot, use more strands of floss; wrap only once.

Fig. 5

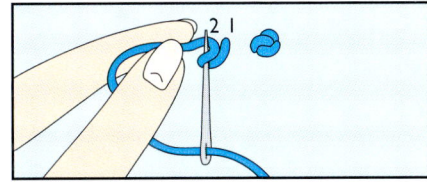

LAZY DAISY STITCH
Bring needle up at 1 and go down at 2 to form a loop; bring needle up at 3, keeping thread below point of needle (Fig. 6a). Go down at 4 to anchor loop (Fig. 6b).

Fig. 6a   Fig. 6b

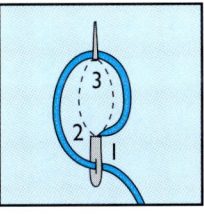 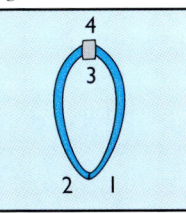

RUNNING STITCH
Make a series of straight stitches with stitch length equal to the space between stitches (Fig. 7).

Fig. 7

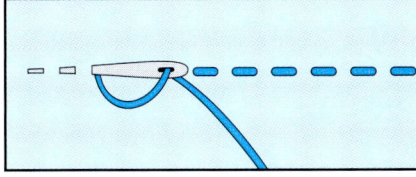

STEM STITCH
Bring needle up at 1. Keeping thread below stitching line, go down at 2 and up at 3. Go down at 4 and up at 5. (Fig. 8).

Fig. 8

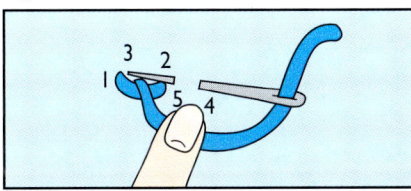

STRAIGHT STITCH
Bring needle up at 1 and go down at 2 (Fig. 9). Length of stitches may be varied as desired.

Fig. 9

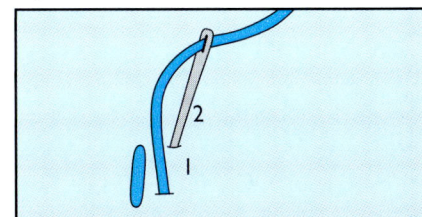

CREDITS

We want to extend a warm *thank you* to the generous people who allowed us to photograph our projects at their homes: Sandra Cook, Jodie Davis, Ellison Poe, Duncan and Nancy Porter, Molly Satterfield, Leighton Weeks, Anne Jarrard, and Tim and Janna Laughlin.

To Wisconsin Technicolor LLC of Pewaukee, Wisconsin, we say thank you for the superb color reproduction and excellent pre-press preparation.

We especially want to thank photographers Mark Mathews, Larry Pennington, Andy Uilkie, and Ken West of Peerless Photography, and Jerry R. Davis of Jerry Davis Photography, all of Little Rock, Arkansas, for their time, patience, and excellent work. Photography stylists Sondra Daniel and Jan Nobles also deserve a special mention for the high quality of their collaboration with these photographers.

Thanks also go to Ruth Ann Epperson, who assisted in testing the projects in this book.